Victorious Bible Curriculum

THE BEGINNING (PART 1 OF 9)
God created a home for mankind, and placed us in it to tend and guard it as His image. When we rebelled, God promised a seed of the woman to one day restore creation — and preserved that seed when our violence filled the world.

THE PATRIARCHS (PART 2 OF 9)
God chose Abraham to be the custodian of the line through which the promised redeemer would come. Abraham's grandson Jacob became the father of the twelve tribes of Israel, a nation that would bless the whole earth.

THE EXODUS (PART 3 OF 9)
For 400 years, God grew Jacob's tiny family into a nation. Through Moses, He released them from slavery to give them a new home. Despite the faithless first generation's rebellion, their children would inherit the promised land.

CONQUEST AND JUDGMENT (PART 4 OF 9)
Under Joshua, the children of the exodus conquered the promised land. After they settled in, they fell into idolatry and suffered under foreign domination. Time after time, they needed God's deliverance through a head-crushing judge.

THE KINGDOM OF ISRAEL (PART 5 OF 9)
God used Israel's first kings, the vacillating Saul and the head-crusher David, to give Israel peace. Solomon built a prosperous kingdom, which then split and fell into idolatry. After 70 years' exile in Babylon, God restored them to the land.

THE COMING OF THE MESSIAH (PART 6 OF 9)
The long wait for the serpent-crushing redeemer came to an end with the birth of Jesus of Nazareth. Raised in Galilee and baptized in the Jordan, He began to proclaim the kingdom of God and demonstrate God's love and power.

THE MINISTRY OF JESUS (PART 7 OF 9)
The blind could see, the sick were healed, the dead raised. The kingdom of God was truly at hand. But the leaders of Israel rejected the One God had sent to save them from their sins and deliver them into God's kingdom.

JESUS' FINAL DAYS (PART 8 OF 9)
On Thursday, before His arrest, Jesus ate one final meal with His disciples. Then He was arrested, beaten, falsely accused, tried, convicted and crucified. But death could not hold Him and the grave could not contain Him.

THE BEGINNING OF THE CHURCH (PART 9 OF 9)
After His resurrection, Jesus' followers received the power of the Holy Spirit to disciple the nations of the world, baptizing them and teaching them all that Jesus had said. Christ's body grew and began to crush the enemy's head under her feet.

Copyright © 2017 by Joe Anderson and Tim Nichols

All rights reserved
Printed in the United States of America
First Edition

No part of this book may be reproduced in any form or by any electronic or mechanical means, including information storage and retrieval systems, except for brief quotations in printed reviews, without the prior permission of the author.

Unless otherwise indicated, all Scripture quotations are taken from the New King James Version®. Copyright © 1982 by Thomas Nelson, Inc. Used by permission. All rights reserved.

Scripture quotations marked (NIV) are taken from the Holy Bible, New International Version®, NIV®. Copyright © 1973, 1978, 1984, 2011 by Biblica, Inc.™ Used by permission of Zondervan. All rights reserved worldwide. www.zondervan.com The "NIV" and "New International Version" are trademarks registered in the United States Patent and Trademark Office by Biblica, Inc.™

Author's translation or paraphrase indicated by an asterisk after the reference.

Illustrations by Gustave Doré
Colorized and modified by William Britton

Praise for Headwaters Bible Curriculum

These lessons are not just a way to teach the Bible to middle school kids. As I read the lessons, I found both my head and my heart irresistibly engaged. Joe and Tim have opened the grace and truth of God's Word in a way that seriously lifts us towards Christ while nudging us outward towards the world. I recommend these studies for both devotional and motivational reading!

Dave Cheadle, President of the Rocky Mountain Classis, Reformed Church of America

While I have spent quite a bit of time studying the Bible myself, I find your ideas and themes to be real food for thought and they help tie together much of the story God is telling throughout... I've already talked with people about your curriculum and have recommended they look into it for their own families. I can't loan out my copy for their perusal, because I'm using it everyday!

Linda Kidder, Home Educator, Colorado

I LOVE THIS BOOK!!!! We're just finishing up the Garden narrative. We've had such fruitful discussions—I have been pleased with it in every way. In fact, I'm hoping our church will start using it. I haven't had any problems or difficulties using the curriculum, I ONLY have good things to say about it. In fact, I'm in danger of writing in all caps I'm so enthusiastic about it.

Leah Robinson, Home Educator, Texas

I am really enjoying having this resource to work from and steer our lessons!

Christy Johnson, Bible Teacher, Bingham Academy, Ethiopia

Our family actually loves the curriculum. My children are in 5th and 8th grade and the content has suited both of their levels perfectly. To this point we hadn't found a curriculum that taught the Bible at such a detailed level that has also kept the kids engaged. We've had to slow down on the materials because otherwise they would be through them well before the school year is up. We are planning on buying the rest of the series.

Chris Turner, Home Educator, Colorado

How to Use This Book

This series of little manuals walks you through the biblical Story from end to end. Just read. Here are a few things you might want to keep in mind as you read through the Story.

- Try to love the characters. God does....
- The story is written in such a way as to make sin look stupid, but remember that the characters are all real people. No matter how stupid the choice, a real person actually looked at the options and then picked that particular one for reasons that seemed pretty good at the time. Nobody gets up in the morning and says, "I'm going to make stupid life choices that people will be mocking for centuries." Try to see it from their point of view. Ask yourself, "Why did this look like a good idea at the time?" That's how you learn to recognize temptations. It's easy to see sinful and stupid choices for what they are in hindsight, but in the moment it's often very hard. So learn to think through what these choices looked like from the inside, in the heat of the moment — you'll be amazed what you learn about yourself.
- Pay attention to the patterns. We'll point out a bunch of them as we go through the Story, but try to spot them yourself, too. If you can learn to read the Word and see the patterns in the Story, you will become able to read the world around you and see the patterns in the story God is telling right now.
- In the Old Testament curriculum, every lesson came with a Psalm. Not all of the New Testament lessons do, but you should know enough about how to connect the Psalms to the Story that you can discover your own connections. If there is no Psalm provided, feel free to take some time to read through a few Psalms and try to find one that fits. You'll be surprised what you can learn.
- As with any book that talks about Scripture, don't necessarily take our word for anything. Imagine you're sitting in a living room or around a campfire with us, and we're just talking about the Story. You're free to disagree, correct, challenge our understanding. The Word is the authority, not us — so grab your Bible and look things up yourself.

You'll find a section labeled "Activities" following the lesson. The point of this section is to immerse you as deeply in the Story as possible, through prayer, meditation on the Story, and other exercises. The "Evaluation" questions at the end of each lesson will help you to check your understanding of the material.

For Small Group Leaders
Have everyone in the group read the lesson ahead of time. Depending on how involved your group is, you can have them engage some or all of the activities, or you can save those for group time when you're together. The evaluation questions might serve as discussion starters if the conversation lags.

Table of Contents

Unit 6 The Church is Born 7
    Lesson 6.1 Pentecost 9
    Lesson 6.2 Peter and the Growing Church 17
    Lesson 6.3 The Stoning of Stephen 23
    Lesson 6.4 The Church Persecuted and Scattered 31
    Lesson 6.5 The Conversion of Saul 39
    Lesson 6.6 The Conversion of Cornelius 45
    Lesson 6.7 Peter's Imprisonment 53
Unit 7 The Church Expands 59
    Lesson 7.1 Paul's First Missionary Journey 61
    Lesson 7.2 The Jerusalem Council 69
    Lesson 7.3 Paul's Second Missionary Journey 77
    Lesson 7.4 Paul's Third Missionary Journey 85
    Lesson 7.5 Paul's Arrest and Journey to Rome 93
Final Activities 105

UNIT 6: THE CHURCH IS BORN

Before He ascended, Jesus told the disciples that He was going to send the Holy Spirit to empower them to bring all nations to Christ. They waited in Jerusalem until the Holy Spirit came on them in power and enabled Peter to boldly preach the gospel in Jerusalem. That day, 3,000 people came to Christ. Peter then led the charge to build the Church in Jerusalem.

The gospel spread quickly throughout the city, but, of course, the religious leaders were opposed to it from the start (after all, they had just killed Jesus for spreading the same message). Peter and John were imprisoned for healing a lame man in the name of Jesus, but were miraculously delivered from prison. But God had a different calling for Stephen, a man full of the Holy Spirit; he was stoned to death by the Sanhedrin for preaching boldly in the name of Jesus.

The religious leaders thought that persecution would dissuade the Christians from spreading their message, but it actually had the opposite effect. On account of the persecution that arose after Stephen was killed, the Church was scattered throughout Judea and Samaria (in keeping with Jesus' commission in Acts 1:8). Philip led the charge to bring the gospel to Samaria, then to Judea. Philip's is the first missionary journey we see in Acts, but there are many more to come.

Meanwhile, Saul, who had been a part of the martyrdom of Stephen, was on his way to Damascus on a mission to stop the spread of the gospel. But he was stopped in his tracks when Jesus appeared to him in a flash of light. God was going to stop the persecutors with the power of His grace, not by the power of the sword.

The gospel had gone out to Judea and Samaria in fulfillment of Jesus' commission in Acts 1:8, but Jesus had said it would go to the ends of the earth. With clear confirmation and direction from the Lord, Peter and Cornelius (a Gentile) met together. Peter preached the gospel to Cornelius and his friends and family. Immediately they received the gift of the Holy Spirit—without even getting circumcised or following the Old Testament Law. This was the beginning of the mission of the Church to the entire world.

Back in Jerusalem, persecution continued to increase. Herod decided that it might be politically expedient to start killing the leaders of the Church. He had James killed and it played well, so he arrested Peter next. While in prison, Peter was miraculously delivered. The way the story is told, Peter experienced a sort of death and resurrection; then the Lord struck Herod dead.

LESSON 6.1

Pentecost

UNIT 6

THE STORY

Lesson Theme - Mission with the miraculous
In this lesson, the story begins of the Church crushing the head of the serpent as she fulfills the great commission to reach the world with the gospel. We are the people of the risen King and the sons and daughters by faith of the apostles; their mission is our mission.

In Acts, Christianity grew from being a small sect of Judaism (120 people) to a worldwide movement. We want to tell this story; but beyond that, we want to see *how* the twelve apostles were so effective at reaching the world and draw out lessons on how we can reach the world around us.

In this lesson, you want to come to grips with how much the early disciples needed the miraculous, and how much we still do. In spreading the gospel to the world, we are not selling a pyramid scheme, and we are not trying to get people to simply buy into a set of beliefs. Rather, we are bringing the living God and His living gospel to those around us. The Church started with a miraculous move of the Holy Spirit on the people of God. We need the same today.

Jesus commissioned the disciples and ascended into heaven
Acts 1:4-8 records an abbreviated version of the great commission (fullest version: Matt 28:16-20). Before Jesus ascended, He reminded the disciples of their job, or mission, on earth: to be witnesses. In Matthew, this mission is spelled out as a threefold calling: to *make disciples* by *baptizing* and *teaching* them to obey Jesus' commands.

OVERVIEW

Jesus commissioned the disciples to go into the world, preach the gospel and bring all nations to Christ. This was an impossible calling for man, but Jesus promised the Holy Spirit would come to empower them to accomplish the mission. When the Holy Spirit came, the 120 Christians spoke in tongues and Peter preached a convicting sermon, leading 3,000 people to Christ. And thus, the Church began.

SOURCE MATERIAL

Acts 1-2

In Acts, the focus is on the power to accomplish the mission, "...you shall receive power when the Holy Spirit has come upon you" (Acts 1:8). The Holy Spirit would fall on the disciples in a few short days to give them power to accomplish the mission.

When Jesus first appeared to the disciples after His resurrection, He breathed on them and they received the Holy Spirit (John 20:23), fulfilling Jesus' promise that He would send the Holy Spirit from the Father (John 15:26-27). In Acts, something different is happening; it doesn't say that they would *receive* the Holy Spirit as they did in John 20; it says that the Holy Spirit would *come upon* them. This same language is used in Judges when the Holy Spirit would *come upon* a judge to accomplish mighty things for the Lord. Additionally, later in Acts, it says that the disciples were *filled* with the Holy Spirit which has

Unit 6: The Church is Born

OBJECTIVES

Feel...

- joy at the outpouring of the Holy Spirit and the beginning of the Christian mission.
- a sense of the scale of Christianity's rapid growth.

Understand...

- that the disciples received the Holy Spirit when Jesus breathed on them in John 20.
- that the gift of the outpouring of the Holy Spirit at Pentecost was to give Christians power to accomplish their mission.
- that the Holy Spirit would come on the disciples multiple times to give them power in specific circumstances.
- that the disciples waited on the Holy Spirit before they started their mission, but they didn't wait lazily; they prepared themselves for the work God was going to do through them.
- that the gift of tongues is the ability to speak in another language.
- that Peter's sermon communicated the gospel to the Israelites who were responsible for killing Jesus.

Apply this understanding by...

- praying for the miraculous.
- waiting diligently.

similar connotations as *come upon* and was used of John the Baptist (Luke 1:15). In other words, the promise given in Acts as Jesus ascended, was a promise to the disciples that the Holy Spirit would come upon them in a special way to allow them to perform miraculous things for the Lord.

This "coming upon" of the Holy Spirit is not as simple as a second blessing theology—the idea that once you have been born again, you also need something called the baptism of the Holy Spirit to effectively serve the Lord. Neither is it something that once you have it, you never need it again. Rather, in Acts we see the Holy Spirit coming upon the apostles and others in times of ministry need so that they could accomplish something that was outside of the their own ability. We need the Holy Spirit to come upon us again and again to enable us to do what He has called us to do. Consider Peter: in Acts 2 the Spirit came upon him, and he preached such that 3,000 were saved. In Acts 4:8, Peter was again filled with the Holy Spirit and preached against the religious leaders. This is the pattern: repeated outpourings of the Spirit to accomplish mighty things for God.

After Jesus gave this commission to His disciples, He ascended to heaven and left them on earth to carry out their mission in the power of the Holy Spirit (Acts 1:9).

The disciples waited for the Holy Spirit
Following Jesus' ascension, the disciples went back to the upper room where they had been staying, to continue to wait for the Holy Spirit to come on them in power. But they didn't wait lazily; they appointed a new apostle to replace Judas (Acts 1:12-26).

We can learn a couple of lessons from the disciples here. First, the disciples waited on the Holy Spirit and didn't get ahead of God, because they knew that without the Holy Spirit, they couldn't spread the gospel of Jesus Christ. But at the same time (and here's the second lesson) waiting doesn't mean doing nothing. While they waited, the disciples prayed. They knew the fire was going to come from heaven; the Holy Spirit would be poured out, so they stacked up wood for the fire.

Pentecost
On the day of Pentecost, the Holy Spirit came upon the disciples in power. A great sound of wind entered the house, tongues of fire descended on the disciples, and they began to speak in tongues—foreign languages (Acts 2:1-4).

This gift of speaking in foreign languages was not just a one-off miracle to come with the outpouring of the Holy Spirit; speaking in tongues becomes a theme in Acts as the gospel spread out from Jerusalem. Neither was this miracle simply a gimmick to get people's attention. There are reasons God chose speaking in tongues as a sign of the gospel.

First, it was an effective miracle because Jerusalem was full of Jewish pilgrims who spoke many different languages and were there to celebrate the Feast of Weeks (Acts 2:5). Speaking in tongues gave the disciples an audience in the city, an audience who would understand the languages and see the miraculous nature of the occurrence. Second, speaking in tongues was a sign of the reversal of Babel. Jesus had been raised from the dead, and God's work of healing all of creation was beginning. At Babel, God confused the people's tongues and scattered them throughout the world. Now, God was making one Church of all peoples in Christ. Finally, the gift of tongues is a sign of the mission of the Church: to go to *all peoples* and make disciples.

Since the city was packed with pilgrims, the disciples easily drew a large crowd. The many pilgrims heard the sound of the rushing wind and a group of 120 people speaking in a variety of languages and came to see what was going on (Acts 2:5-6). They were amazed, because they could all hear these disciples speaking in their own languages. Some people, however, mocked them and said they were drunk.

Peter's sermon
Peter saw his opportunity to preach the gospel and stood up to explain to the crowds what was going on. He pointed out that they were not drunk—that would be an odd thing to happen at nine in the morning. Rather, they were fulfilling Joel's prophecy that God's people would do all sorts of wondrous things in the last days (Acts 2:16-21).

The rest of Peter's sermon in Acts 2:14-39 can be summarized as follows: "What you are seeing is a sign that Jesus is not dead, but alive. God allowed Him to die and raised Him to life; that was God's plan. We know this because David said that the Messiah would not be abandoned to the grave, but would be raised to new life in God's presence (Ps 16). David went to the grave and remains there, but Jesus ascended to God's right hand as David prophesied in Psalm 110. Jesus is the Messiah—and you (Jews) killed Him. But if you repent and are baptized, you will be forgiven and receive the gift of the Holy Spirit."

The sermon was straightforward and convicting. Peter was not just asking them to believe in Jesus; he was asking them to believe in Jesus *and* repent of killing the Messiah. And it worked; about 3,000 people believed, repented and were baptized that day (Acts 2:41).

The new Church
The Church, now numbering 3,120 was still a relatively small segment of Jerusalem's population, and it was made up mostly of Jews who lived outside of Jerusalem and even Israel. By all appearances, many of these converts stayed in Jerusalem, at least for a while. This meant that there were a number of people without homes, without much money and new to the Christian

faith. In order to survive and provide for their own, the Church had to chip in and provide for each other. And so they shared with one another—they "had all things in common" (Acts 2:44). They made space in their lives for lots of teaching, fellowship, communion and prayer; and they did it all in the context of a tight-knit community.

There is an important piece to get here that is often overlooked. In addition to meeting daily in the temple, they also broke bread in their homes, or households (Acts 2:46). In Jerusalem at the time, and throughout the Roman empire, the household (*oikos* in Greek) was the fundamental building block of society. A household was not a nuclear family like we have today with a few kids, parents and a dog. A Greco-Roman household consisted of 20-50 people including an extended family as well as slaves or servants. Households were economic and family units that lived life together—they depended on each other, fellowshipped together and worshiped together. Christianity grew incredibly fast by spreading from household to household throughout the Roman empire. We will return to this concept throughout the remainder of the lessons in Acts to learn how Christianity spread.

Observations

At this point in its development, Christianity wasn't a worldwide religion; the Church was made entirely of a group of Jews in Jerusalem who believed that Jesus was the Messiah. Peter's sermon was specifically addressed to the people gathered in Jerusalem as Jews. They worshipped at the temple; they followed the Law—they were good Jews. In fact, it is possible that the disciples didn't yet understand that they would bring the gospel to the Gentiles. In the following chapters of Acts, many Jewish paradigms and ways of doing things would have to be broken before Christianity would become a religion on its own.

The Christians were a sect of Judaism, but they were the *true* sect. God really did send His Son to His own people, and they really did reject and kill Him. The generation of Israel who rejected the Messiah was under God's judgement, and their destruction was coming (Rome sacked Jerusalem in A.D. 70). Therefore, the gospel took a particular shape for the early Christians talking to the Jews in Jerusalem and even outside Jerusalem as they spread out: "Israel is responsible for killing the Messiah; repent, and you will be saved from the judgement coming upon you."

APPLICATION

The big application from this lesson is that we need the miraculous involvement of the Holy Spirit to accomplish the mission that Jesus has called us to. God still does miracles; He heals the sick, casts out demons and much more. As you go out to do your mission, do it in a spirit of prayer. Pray for little miracles and pray for big miracles. By little miracles, pray for God to provide gospel encounters with unbelievers (obvious opportunities to speak gospel truth into people's lives); pray that He would give more opportunities for relationships to develop. Big miracles are great, but the little ones are where daily ministry happens for most people most of the time.

There are times of waiting, times when God doesn't want us to share the gospel with particular people, times when we should simply develop relationships and develop ourselves. Sometimes we need to wait, but not do nothing—these are the times to get ourselves prepared for when God will do more.

Unit 6: The Church is Born

ACTIVITIES

1. How to Wait. Read through Acts 1:12-26. In the space below, make a list of all the things the disciples did while they waited for the outpouring of the Holy Spirit. _____
_____
_____
_____
_____
_____
_____

In many ways you may also be in a period of waiting in your life; you may not yet know what your specific gifting and calling are. In the space below, make a list of some things you can do to wait wisely until you really know and act upon your calling._____
_____
_____
_____
_____

2. Journal Time: Pray for Miracles. Spend some time in prayer, asking God to reveal ways you can be praying for miracles. These prayers may be requests for opportunities to share the gospel or pray for unbelievers, prayers for peace during difficult times, or prayers for God's provision. Make your prayer requests specific, pray faithfully for these miracles and thank God for them when they happen._____
_____
_____
_____
_____
_____
_____

Lesson 6.1

EVALUATION

1. What happened to the disciples when Jesus breathed on them in John 20? _____
_____
_____
_____

2. What is the difference between Jesus breathing on the disciples in John 20 and the outpouring of the Holy Spirit on Pentecost? _____
_____
_____
_____

3. What did the disciples do while they waited for the Holy Spirit to come upon them? _____
_____
_____

4. What is the gift of tongues in Acts 2? _____
_____
_____

5. Why do you think God might have given them that particular gift? _____
_____
_____

6. What was Peter's sermon all about? _____
_____
_____
_____

7. How many converted when Peter preached this sermon? _____

   What happened with all of these new converts? _____
_____
_____

LESSON 6.2

Peter and the Growing Church

UNIT 6

THE STORY

Lesson Theme - God used miracles to spread the gospel, but the Church needed encouragement when Peter and John were imprisoned.

At Pentecost, God began bringing new life to the world. The world was lost in the fall, but God was claiming that ground for His kingdom. And He did it with miracles performed by His followers in the power of the Spirit. We saw this in Acts 2 when Peter preached a convicting sermon; the response was overwhelming and accompanied by signs and wonders. The apostles knew exactly what was happening; Jesus had prepared them for their mission, and they were ready to boldly preach the gospel. But the Church as a whole was perhaps more fragile and needed more confirmation that God was truly at work. In Acts 3, Peter and John healed a lame man and preached the gospel to a crowd of people again, but this time the response was not as good. They were arrested and imprisoned.

The question that this narrative poses is, "Who has more power: the Church and her mission, or the civil and religious authorities in this world?" If the power of the gospel can be quenched by passing laws, throwing people into prison or burning Bibles, then Christ died in vain. Now, for Peter, the answer to this question was obvious; he knew the gospel was going to win, and this knowledge gave him incredible boldness before the council and great confidence when released. But the fragile, newborn Church was looking for confirmation that God was behind them, and He delivered.

OVERVIEW

Peter and John were imprisoned overnight for healing a lame man in the name of Jesus. The next day, a council of the religious leaders in Jerusalem convened to question them about this healing. Peter boldly proclaimed before the council that they healed the man in the name of Jesus whom those very religious leaders were guilty of crucifying. The council deliberated about what to do, but they were trapped. They could not deny the healing, since everyone knew about it, and they could not punish Peter and John for healing a lame man, so they decided to threaten and release them. Upon their release, Peter and John returned to their companions who immediately thought of Psalm 2 and began to pray. After they prayed, the house shook by the power of the Holy Spirit, and the Church redoubled their efforts in fellowship and mission.

SOURCE MATERIAL

- Acts 3-4
- Psalm 2
- Proverbs 30:5-6

Notice that it was the priests, captains of the temple, and the Sadducees who arrested and put Peter and John on trial (Acts 4:1-3). These were, perhaps, some of the same people who put our Lord on trial when He healed someone on the Sabbath and the same people who led the charge to crucify Him. They thought they had

Unit 6: The Church is Born

OBJECTIVES

Feel...

- excited about the ongoing confirmation and victory of the newly founded Church.
- thankful for the vindication that our Lord Jesus received before the same people who crucified Him.

Understand...

- that the body of Christ was performing the work of Christ on the earth.
- that Peter and John were filling the role of Jesus in this story.
- that God was confirming the Church in its calling and mission.

Apply this understanding by...

- considering times in your life when singing Psalm 2 would be an appropriate response to a gospel victory.
- considering times when fear prevented you from being bold for the gospel.
- thinking of who you should be sharing the gospel with but isn't due to lack of boldness.

put this whole Jesus problem behind them when they killed Him; but here His followers were starting a whole movement claiming that Jesus had raised from the dead. The council's hands were tied, however; if they thought it would help, they could simply kill Peter and John, but a large crowd had just seen them heal a lame man, and not even the council could deny it. Notice how similar this story is to John 9 when Jesus healed the man born blind; Peter and John, Jesus' followers, were playing the part of Jesus defeating the enemy.

After deliberating a while, the council decided the best course of action was to threaten Peter and John and release them; any other response would only make the council's problem worse. Peter told them they would continue to preach the gospel anyway; it was right to obey God rather than men. So the council threatened them some more and released them (Acts 4:16-21).

When Peter and John told their companions their story, they responded by quoting (or perhaps singing) Psalm 2 (Acts 4:23-26). They realized that this was a Psalm 2 moment. Play this up; when was the last time you saw the gospel victorious over serious opposition, and everyone responded by saying, "Whoa, this reminds me of Psalm 2!"? To put it simply, Jesus was now ruling from the heavenly Zion (Ps 2:6), and the heathen nations attempted to make war against Him (Ps 2:1-2), but God laughed because He was giving the nations to His Son as an inheritance (Ps 2:8). Peter and John were living this story; they were making disciples of the nations (making them into a fit inheritance for Christ), and the civil authorities tried to stop them.

After realizing that they were in the midst of a Psalm 2 kind of moment, the disciples prayed. They prayed fervently that they would have boldness even when threatened by these "heathen nations" that made war against them. They prayed that the Spirit would show up and enable them to perform signs and miracles through the name of the Lord Jesus. In response, the Holy Spirit shook the house, a not so subtle reminder that He was with them no matter what challenge they faced.

Acts 4 ends with a description of the Church's unity—the "multitude of those who believed were of one heart and one soul" (Acts 4:32). Having been encouraged by the release of Peter and John and the Spirit's presence among them, they doubled down on their mission and unity.

APPLICATION

The practical application for this lesson is that you live in a world where there is genuine and strong opposition to the gospel. It sometimes comes from civil authorities, sometimes from unbelieving friends or sometimes from the pressure of our culture. But regardless where it comes from, the opposition is there. In other words, there are serpents in the world: those who hate God and the gospel and want to put a stop to His work. However, Jesus is risen from the dead; the serpent has been and is being defeated. Psalm 2 still applies; the efforts of the heathen nations to take a stand against the Lord, the Messiah, or the Church, the body of Christ, are just vain rage; God laughs at them. We can and must be bold in the calling that God has given us; victory is assured, the war has been won. God is "a shield to those who put their trust in Him" (Prov 30:5-6).

ACTIVITIES

1. Reflection: Psalm 2 and What's Your Story? When the Church heard about Peter and John's victory against the council, they immediately began quoting Psalm 2. Reflect on the significance of this psalm. Then, think of a story from your life or a story from Church history where Psalm 2 would have been an appropriate song to sing in response. Write this story in the space below and explain why Psalm 2 would be an appropriate psalm in this situation.

Unit 6: The Church is Born

2. Journal Time: Boldness for the Gospel. Consider whom God has placed in your life to share Christ's love with. Have you been bold in sharing the gospel, or has fear stopped you from doing so? Spend some time writing about this in the space below. Then ask God for opportunities to share the gospel with this person and boldness to do so when these opportunities arise.

Lesson 6.2

EVALUATION

1. What happened that led to Peter and John getting arrested? _____
_____
_____

2. What was it that bothered the religious leaders most about the healing? _____
_____
_____
_____

3. Why were the religious leaders not able to punish Peter and John? _____
_____
_____

4. What did Peter say when the religious leaders told them not to preach the name of Jesus? _____
_____
_____

5. Why did the Church sing Psalm 2 in response to what happened? _____
_____
_____
_____

6. Are you as bold as Peter is in sharing the gospel? Why or why not? _____
_____

LESSON 6.3

The Stoning of Stephen

UNIT 6

THE STORY

Lesson Theme - Boldness and suffering advanced the mission of the Church.

As the gospel went out in Jerusalem, it provoked a strong response from the Jewish religious leaders. They wanted this Jesus movement stopped yesterday; in fact, they thought they killed it off when they killed Jesus! But no, God's people continued to preach the gospel with the same boldness as Jesus Christ had, and it provoked the same kind of response from the religious leaders—violence. When Stephen used the whole weight of Israel's history to bring conviction upon the Sanhedrin, they treated him the same way they had treated Christ—they persecuted him. This persecution, however, did not mean the beginning of the end of Christianity; it meant the beginning of its expansion.

Background

Getting the background details right will help you understand the importance of these events to the continuing story of the spread of the Church through the book of Acts.

As one of the first deacons in the Church, Stephen was a significant figure. The point of conflict which made it necessary for the apostles to appoint deacons gives us some perspective on the nature of the infant Church. As we saw in Acts 2, a large number of non-resident Jews became believers.

The Church had been growing rapidly and it had been growing in two ways. First, many Jews who were visiting from out of town, even the Helle-

OVERVIEW

The Church was born into a volatile situation in Jerusalem. Many of the Jewish believers who had lived in Greek cultures (known as Hellenistic Jews), were just visiting Jerusalem when they heard the gospel. Many of these new Christians stayed in Jerusalem, which meant there was a need to share resources, food and living space and to take care of all the new believers. Unfortunately, some of the Hellenistic widows were being neglected. So the apostles appointed deacons to distribute the food fairly. Stephen, a Hellenist himself, was chosen as a deacon. He got into a dispute with some non-Christian Hellenistic Jews who falsely accused him and took him before the Sanhedrin. Stephen preached a convicting message against the religious leaders and was killed for it. His face shone like Moses, and he died innocent like Jesus. Stephen's death was the beginning of the expansion of the gospel in keeping with Jesus' commission in Acts 1:8.

SOURCE MATERIAL

- Acts 6-7

nists, were turning to the Lord. This was perhaps where a bulk of the converts written of in Acts 2 came from. Second, Acts 6 reveals that many of the priests were coming to the Lord as well.

This meant that the Church was made up of a number of local Jews, including some priests, as well as a number of Hellenistic Jews. Hellenistic

Unit 6: The Church is Born

OBJECTIVES

Feel...

- awe at Stephen's boldness in proclaiming the gospel before the religious leaders.
- gratitude that God powerfully uses even those who don't "fit the mold."

Understand...

- the complicated dynamics in a Jerusalem church made up of permanent resident Jewish Christians as well as Hellenistic Jews residing there temporarily.
- that the Church needed deacons to keep up with serving the Hellenistic Jews who were being neglected.
- that the deacons they chose were not *just* servants, but great men of God.
- that Stephen was a Hellenistic deacon.
- the main point of Stephen's sermon: that the Sanhedrin killed God's prophet (Jesus) just like Israel's religious leaders had always killed the prophets.
- the meaning of the phrase "cut to the heart" and the connection to Acts 2.
- how Stephen was bearing the image of both Jesus and Moses in this passage.

Apply this understanding by...

- believing that when we are faithful as Stephen was faithful, God can use us in surprising ways.

Jews were those who lived throughout the Roman empire and had adopted a Greek lifestyle. Many of these Jews were in Jerusalem for the feast, became Christians, and apparently stuck around. As a result, they had to find places to live and food to eat. As we saw in Lesson 6.1, the Church pooled resources and took care of each other.

However, as time went on, the widows of the Hellenistic Christians were being overlooked in favor of the Jewish widows (Acts 6:1). So the apostles appointed deacons (servants) to take care of the distribution of food so the apostles could focus on word and prayer.

It should be noted that Stephen is a Greek name, and in all likelihood, he was a Hellenist. He also wasn't just an administrator, making sure food was distributed fairly. He did that, but he was also full of the Holy Spirit and a powerful miracle-worker.

Stephen's sermon
As it happened, Stephen created quite the controversy. Hellenistic Jews who had *not* converted to Christianity began to argue with him (Acts 6:9). They convinced some other men to bear false witness against Stephen, which drew the attention of the elders and teachers of the law (these were local Jews, perhaps the same people who had been responsible for bringing accusation against Jesus). These religious leaders brought Stephen before the Sanhedrin—the rulers in Jerusalem who had been responsible for convicting Jesus. Stephen had worked his way up the food chain, causing offense to everyone along the way.

When Stephen was questioned by the high priest, he took the opportunity to preach a sermon, one that walked through the entire narrative of Israel, before getting to the call to repentance at the end. The picture here is truly amazing; Stephen, a foreign, Hellenistic Jew, standing before the highest Jewish council in Jerusalem, preaching to them!

Lets take a close look at Stephen's sermon (recorded in Acts 7:1-53). There are several important points here.

Stephen started by drawing attention to God's promise to Abraham (Acts 7:2-8). God told Abraham to leave his homeland and go to a land God would show him. Abraham obeyed, and when he arrived in Canaan, God made a promise to him: his descendants would possess the land of Canaan. But first they would be sent down to Egypt to be slaves for 400 years before God would deliver them.

This was the basic hope for all Israel throughout the Old Testament—they would receive their inheritance from God. But what did Israel do when God sent a deliverer to bring them to the promised land? Stephen continued...

When they were enslaved in Egypt, God heard their cry and raised up Moses to deliver them (Acts 7:20). When he was grown, Moses visited his people and saw an Egyptian beating an Israelite, so he killed the Egyptian. The next day, he saw two Israelites fighting and went to break them up. Moses (as Stephen argued) expected that the Israelites would see him as a deliverer sent by God, but they responded by saying, "Who made you a ruler and a judge over us? Do you want to kill me as you did the Egyptian yesterday?" (Acts 7:27-28). When Moses finally led Israel out of the land of Egypt with many miraculous signs, Israel disobeyed him anyway—validating their earlier sentiment, "Who made you a ruler and a judge over us?" The Israelites worshiped an Egyptian idol while Moses met with God at Sinai.

Stephen was drawing attention to a pattern in Israel's history of which the Israelites' response to Moses is the archetypical example: they rejected the prophets God sent to fulfill His promise to bless them.

Moses told Israel that God would send them another prophet like him—a greater one who would bring ultimate fulfillment for Israel in regard to the promises made to Abraham. Stephen implicitly raised the question, "Would Israel reject the final prophet (Jesus Christ) as they had rejected Moses?"

Israel rejected Moses, God's prophet, in spite of God's presence with them in the ark of the covenant, a presence that continued with them into the land when Solomon finally built the temple. And of course, they continued to reject God's prophets in spite of God's presence with them.

This is where the punch line of Stephen's sermon came in: Stephen turned the whole weight of the narrative he just set up against the Sanhedrin: "You stiff-necked and uncircumcised in heart and ears! You always resist the Holy Spirit; as your fathers did, so do you. Which of the prophets did your fathers not persecute? And they killed those who foretold the coming of the Just One, of whom you now have become the betrayers and murderers" (Acts 7:51-52).

With that, they were "cut to the heart" (Acts 7:54) and killed him. The phrase "cut to the heart" is not new in Acts; when Peter preached in Acts 2, his audience was "cut to the heart" as well (Acts 2:37), but Peter's audience repented. And Stephen's sermon was not all that different than Peter's. Both sermons ended with the same punch line: *you are guilty of killing Jesus.* But when Peter preached, the people were convicted and repented, and when Stephen preached, the Sanhedrin were convicted, but they did not repent. When understood clearly by those who hear it, the gospel provokes strong responses—repentance in some and violence in others.

Stephen, like Jesus and Moses
The story of Stephen parallels, in remarkable ways, the story of Jesus. Like Jesus, Stephen was performing miracles and speaking with wisdom. Like in Jesus' story, the religious leaders induced some people to bear false witness against him (Acts 6:13). Like Jesus, Stephen stood before the Sanhedrin under trial by the testimony of false witnesses. And, like Jesus, he calmly bore the accusations and responded gracefully. Finally, like Jesus, Stephen was unjustly killed.

Furthermore, Stephen was like Moses. The irony here is that the accusation brought against him was that he was speaking blasphemy against Moses and against God (Acts 6:11). But when Stephen stood before the Sanhedrin, Acts tells us that his face shone like an angel (Acts 6:15), much like Moses' face had when he came down from Sinai after being in the presence of God. Furthermore, the leaders of Israel rejected Stephen's testimony just as they had rejected Moses' testimony.

Stephen stoned
When Stephen's attackers finally had enough, we are presented with an *almost* humorous scene (Acts 7:54-58a). His convicting sermon made them so mad that they began to gnash their teeth at him. Stephen, unphased by the scene, looked up and saw Jesus at the right hand of God. Then his attackers covered their ears, yelled loudly, ran at him and stoned him to death. Like Jesus, Stephen prayed that God would forgive those who were attacking him.

This story also introduces us to Saul, who will play a major role in the later part of the book of Acts. Saul was not a member of the Sanhedrin and did not, therefore, participate in the actual stoning; but he was close enough to this group of men that he held their coats while they killed Stephen (Acts 7:58b). This scene foreshadows both Saul's persecution of Christians in coming chapters and also the fact that one day he would be on the receiving end of much persecution. He himself would be stoned more than once.

APPLICATION

Stephen was an inspiring leader. He wasn't from the right family; he was a Hellenistic Jew. Furthermore, he was the first martyr, but he wasn't even an apostle. Being a deacon was an important position and demonstrates that Stephen had the support and blessing of the apostles. It was a position that he was qualified for by being spiritual, wise and faithful. The Lord used him mightily because he was willing to hear and obey the Spirit and because he was willing to be bold.

The application here is not to pursue martyrdom. If God brings that along, so be it. The goal is to grow into the kind of people God can use. And God uses those who are faithful over the long run, who listen to the Spirit, develop wisdom and are willing to be bold. God doesn't require that you fit the mold people expect a good Christian to look like; He only requires faithfulness.

Lesson 6.3

ACTIVITIES

1. Compare and Contrast. Stephen's sermon (Acts 6:8-7:52) bears a lot of similarities to Peter's sermon (Acts 2). Read through the passages and make a list of similarities and differences between the two sermons.

Similarities	Differences

Unit 6: The Church is Born

2. Study the Story. Read Stephen's sermon before the Sanhedrin in Acts 7:1-53 and answer the following questions.

What was the promise that God had made to Abraham?_____
_____
_____
_____

Why did God send Moses to the people of Israel?_____
_____
_____
_____

Did Israel receive Moses?_____
_____
_____
_____

What promise did Stephen point to?_____
_____
_____
_____

What was the punch line, the big point, Stephen ended with? _____
_____
_____
_____

Lesson 6.3

EVALUATION

1. What was going on in Jerusalem that necessitated appointing deacons? _____
_____
_____
_____

2. How did Stephen end up on trial before the Sanhedrin? _____
_____
_____
_____

4. What does the phrase "cut to the heart" mean? Talk about Acts 2 in your answer. _____
_____
_____
_____

5. In what ways was Stephen like Jesus? _____
_____
_____
_____

LESSON 6.4

The Church Persecuted and Scattered

UNIT 6

THE STORY

Lesson Theme - The spread of the gospel
In the beginning of Acts, Luke records Jesus' commission to the disciples; they were to be "witnesses to Me in Jerusalem, and in all Judea and Samaria, and to the end of the earth" (Acts 1:8). The gospel is *expansive*—it couldn't stay in Jerusalem; it had to go out. Up until Stephen's martyrdom, the gospel had remained in Jerusalem, but Stephen's death and increasing persecution, in God's wisdom, caused the gospel to proceed from Jerusalem to the ends of the earth.

Philip was the first evangelist, and his remarkable success throughout Samaria and Judea paved the way for the expansion of the gospel. He foreshadowed Paul's later mission throughout the Roman empire.

Saul persecuted the Church
Saul was born for a purpose; he was the kind of person who would go from house to house, motivating Christians to get out and spread the gospel. He even managed to do this before his conversion, working against Christianity instead of for it. When persecution broke out against Christianity, Saul was there smiling approvingly... "At that time a great persecution arose against the church which was at Jerusalem; and they were all scattered throughout the regions of Judea and Samaria, except the apostles" (Acts 8:1). Shortly thereafter, Saul led the charge to persecute the Church throughout the region and was therefore largely responsible for the expansion of the Church as Christians fled from the persecution (Acts 8:3).

OVERVIEW

Up until the martyrdom of Stephen, the gospel had basically stayed in Jerusalem. But after Stephen's death, a great persecution began against Christians, and the Church was scattered throughout Judea and Samaria (in keeping with Jesus' commission in Acts 1:8). We see the expansion of the gospel through the story of Philip's ministry, first in Samaria—healing, preaching and baptizing—and next in Judea where the Ethiopian eunuch was converted on his way home. Philip's is the first missionary journey we see in Acts, but there are many more to come. In fact, Philip was a precursor to the great missionary Paul.

SOURCE MATERIAL

- Acts 8

Philip in Samaria and Judea
The gospel moved from Jerusalem to Judea and Samaria, as Jesus had foretold; and the first stories we get from the mission field are about Philip. Philip was a deacon, appointed along with Stephen; and like Stephen, he was most likely a Hellenistic Jew (a Jew who grew up in Greek culture and lived a Greek-culture lifestyle). And again, like Stephen, Philip was no lightweight. He was a great performer of miracles and was known to cast out demons (Acts 7).

When the persecution began, Philip went to a city in Samaria and began to preach the gospel, cast out demons and heal the sick. His ministry

Unit 6: The Church is Born

OBJECTIVES

Feel...

- excited at the quick advance of the gospel as Philip preached in Judea and Samaria.

Understand...

- that increasing persecution caused the Church to go out of Jerusalem into Judea and Samaria in fulfillment of Jesus' commission in Acts 1:8.
- that Philip and his ministry in Judea and Samaria prefigured Paul's missionary journeys among the Gentiles.
- that Philip (like Stephen) was a Hellenistic deacon and a powerful performer of miracles.
- that Philip brought the gospel to Samaria.
- that Samaritans weren't exactly Gentiles, nor were they Jews; the gospel would more clearly go to the Gentiles later.
- that the Ethiopian eunuch was probably a proselyte, or even an Ethiopian Jew.
- that the Ethiopian was baptized immediately after he believed; this is the pattern in Acts.

Apply this understanding by...

- using your God-given gifts for God's purposes in your life, understanding that there is no such thing as a neutral life.
- evaluating your life to see if you are out in the world on mission for God.

was so effective, that it says there "was great joy in that city" (Acts 8:8).

While Philip was in Samaria, many believed and were baptized. In fact, so many were baptized that word got back to Jerusalem, and the apostles came to visit (Acts 8:14). Interestingly enough, though the gospel had gone out and many believed, they had not received the Holy Spirit. Apparently, the Lord had entrusted the apostles to bring about the outpouring of the Spirit to each new location that the gospel went in this early phase of evangelism. When the apostles (Peter and John) arrived in Samaria, they prayed and laid hands on the new believers, causing them to receive the Holy Spirit (Acts 8:15-6).

A local sorcerer, Simon, who had the respect of the city before Philip arrived, lost his high stature in the city because Philip's miracles were far beyond his petty sorcery. But even this man became a believer.

When Peter and John began laying hands on the new believers, causing them to receive the Holy Spirit, Simon saw a power that could earn his status in the city back. So he tried to buy that power from the apostles! Peter rebuked him, and Simon repented (Acts 8:18-24). Simon's response to the gospel gives us a glimpse of the power the gospel had to turn the world upside down everywhere it went.

It says next that an angel of the Lord told Philip to move south to the road that traveled from Jerusalem to Gaza, and Philip obeyed. There he met an important Ethiopian eunuch (Acts 8:27).

The eunuch was ready to receive the gospel and did so with great joy. He believed and was immediately baptized (Acts 8:36-38). It is important to note this pattern of baptism in Acts: baptism always happened immediately after conversion. Luke draws our attention to this pattern, so

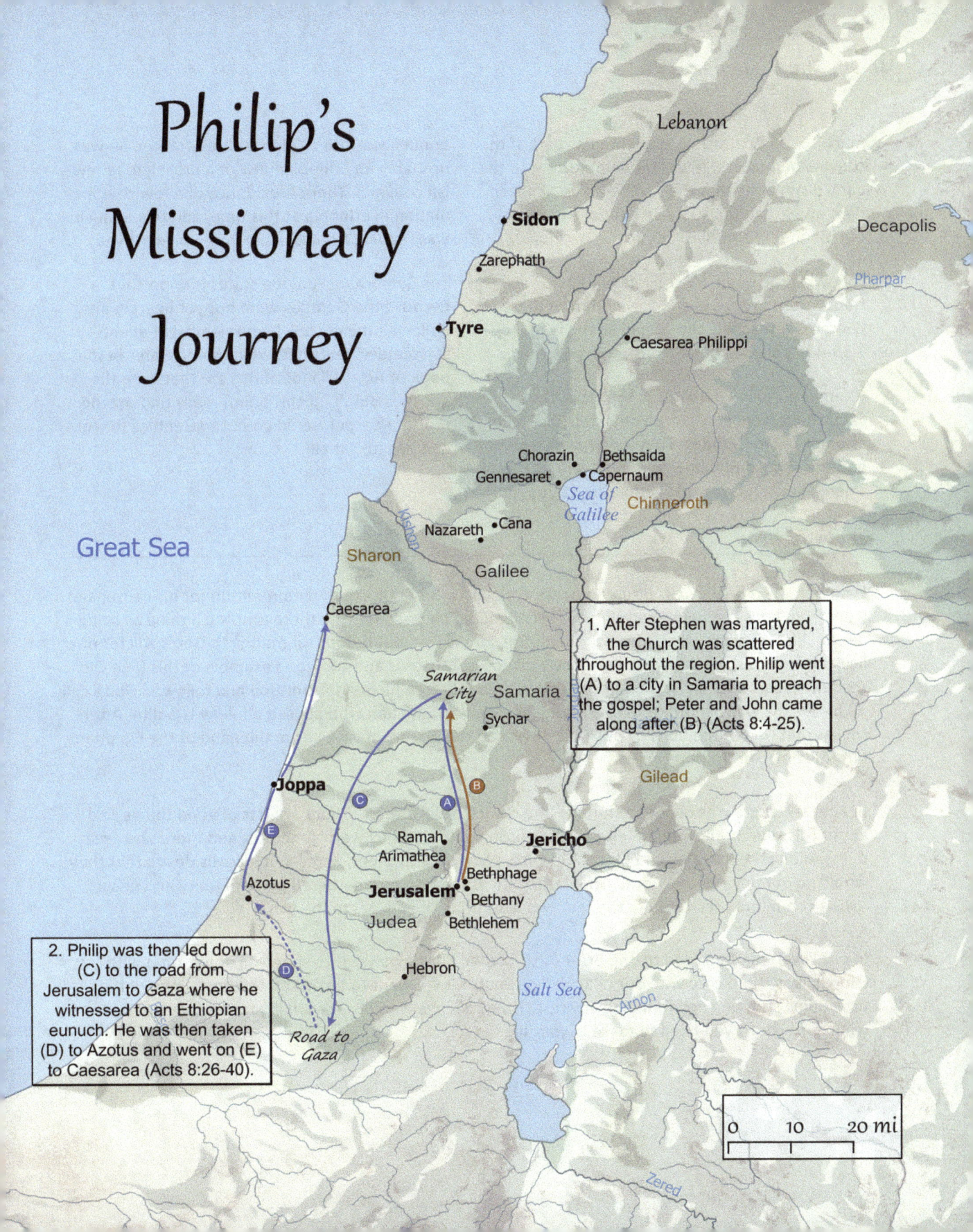

much so, that baptism is presented as part of the conversion process. It was more important to the early evangelists that their converts be baptized right away than that they be baptized in an official manner in a public setting.

Following the eunuch's conversion, Philip was transported to Azotus and traveled from there to Caesarea, preaching the gospel all the way (Acts 8:39-40). This was quite a missionary journey.

As an important side note, to the Jews, the Samaritans were considered outsiders, but were also not called Gentiles. They worshiped Yahweh, had the Torah and followed it, but were not considered Jews. It is also likely that the Ethiopian eunuch was not a Gentile either; rather, he was probably an Ethiopian Jew or a proselyte (a Jewish convert). There is evidence of a Jewish population in Ethiopia at this time, and this eunuch was reading from Isaiah before Philip arrived.

The Samaritans' unique status is important because the Gentiles were not yet hearing and believing the gospel. Some significant events surrounded that shift, which comes later in the book of Acts. All indications are that even the apostles didn't, at this point, really understand that the gospel would go out to Gentiles (Greeks and pagans) at all.

APPLICATION

Even before he believed in Jesus, Saul was zealous for his faith, created momentum for his cause, and went from house to house carrying out his mission. The lesson is that there is no such thing as living a neutral life. We were all created to accomplish something, but before submitting to God's will for our lives, our actions will be twisted unto evil purposes. Moses is another good example of this (See Old Testament Lesson 5.1). He was a born deliverer, but before he heard from God and followed God's call on his life, he was a murderous deliverer—he killed an Egyptian who abused a fellow Israelite. After Moses met God at the burning bush, he delivered the people of Israel from the hand of the Egyptians, but this time, on God's terms.

In Acts 1-7, there was only one church—the church at Jerusalem. There are lots of good things said about this church: they held their possessions in common, they were generous, and there was great unity among the apostles and elders. God was pleased with them; and yet, it was His desire that they would go out unto all the world. God desires the Church to be a gathered place of unity and peace AND a community scattered to the four winds to bring the gospel to the world.

In our lives, we often tend to one error or the other. Either we want to spend all of our time with our church, warm and cozy with our peaceful in-group. Or we want to be out on the front-lines all the time doing stuff and never finding any rest. The challenge is to discern what you tend toward and what corrections you need to make in your life.

Lesson 6.4

ACTIVITIES

1. Compare and Contrast. Fill in the following chart, listing the similarities and differences between Philip and Saul.

Similarities	Differences

What are some lessons you can take away from these similarities and differences? _____
_____
_____
_____
_____
_____
_____

2. Journal Time: Scattered and Gathered. The Church is called to be both the scattered and the gathered people of God. Use the matrix and the questions on the following page to evaluate your own tendencies and temptations.

Unit 6: The Church is Born

Cozy life – lots of time with God's people, rarely on mission

Fruitful life – cycle between gathering and scattering (work and rest)

Gathered – in worship

Scattered – on mission

Death – separated from God's people and God's mission

Stressed life – always doing, never resting

Are you the kind of person who tends toward the gathered community of God and neglects your mission? _____

What kind of temptations will that kind of person experience in their Christian life? _____
_____
_____

Are you the kind of person who likes to be doing stuff for God all the time and rarely pulls back to rest with God's people? _____

What kind of temptations will that kind of person experience in their Christian life? _____
_____
_____

What are some concrete steps you can take to move to a balanced and fruitful life? _____
_____
_____
_____
_____

Lesson 6.4

EVALUATION

1. What did it take for the Church to begin spreading the gospel throughout Judea and Samaria as Jesus had called them to in Acts 1:8? _____
_____
_____

2. Describe how the story of Philip's travels and ministry points to Saul's future ministry. _____
_____
_____
_____
_____

3. What was Stephen's background and position in the Jerusalem church? _____
_____

4. Why do you think that God chose Hellenistic deacons to be on the front lines of the gospel expansion while the apostles remained at Jerusalem? After all, didn't Philip have important work to do in Jerusalem? _____
_____
_____
_____
_____
_____
_____

5. Were the Samaritans and the Ethiopian eunuch Gentiles? Explain your answer. _____
_____
_____

6. Philip left Jerusalem to spread the gospel. Why did Saul leave Jerusalem? _____
_____

LESSON 6.5

The Conversion of Saul

UNIT 6

THE STORY

Lesson Theme - God converted an enemy of the gospel.

Ever since Stephen's death, Philip had been on the front lines of Christian mission, seeking to spread Christianity as far as he could out of Jerusalem. Saul, on the other hand, was in containment mode. He was seeking authorization to head to Damascus so he could start rounding up Christians in order to bring them back to Jerusalem. He wanted to stop the spread of Christianity (Acts 9:1-2). But God had a different plan. Instead of destroying this enemy of the gospel, Jesus spoke to him and he was converted. Immediately Saul repented and became a missionary, but he didn't have nearly the success in mission that Philip had, and an implied contrast is set up. Philip was received everywhere he went, while Saul was attacked.

Saul's conversion

The story of Saul's conversion contrasts nicely with the conversion of the Ethiopian eunuch. Both Saul and the eunuch were traveling along a road when they were converted. The eunuch was reading his Bible; he was seeking God. He knew he was blind and wanted Philip to guide him into the truth and open his eyes. Saul, on the other hand, was out to persecute Christians; he thought he could see, but he really was blind. God saves those who seek Him, but also seeks those who don't know they are lost.

As Saul traveled to Damascus, Jesus appeared to him with a flash of light and asked him, "Saul, Saul, why are you persecuting Me?" (Acts 9:4).

OVERVIEW

Saul was on a missionary journey to persecute Christians when he met Christ in a flash of light. After Jesus spoke to Saul, his heart was open to the truth of the gospel, but his eyes were blinded. He went on to Damascus where he met Ananias, was baptized, and his eyes were opened. Immediately, Saul began preaching the gospel, though to little great effect. Finally, he journeyed to Jerusalem and made peace with the apostles, laying the groundwork for a powerful ministry.

SOURCE MATERIAL

- Acts 9:1-31

Saul responded by asking, "Who are You, Lord?" (Acts 9:5). Saul immediately knew that whoever was speaking to him was his Master, his God, but he didn't know who He was. Unlike the eunuch who eagerly sought and confessed Jesus as Lord, Saul reluctantly confessed when he met his Master face-to-face.

Saul had his spiritual eyes opened when he met Jesus, but he was blinded by the light of Christ. The eunuch knew he needed someone to guide him to the truth (Acts 8:31), but Saul didn't know his blindness until Jesus appeared to him, and then his companions had to guide him into Damascus.

In Damascus, Saul had hands laid on him, was baptized and filled with the Holy Spirit. He was

39

Unit 6: The Church is Born

OBJECTIVES

Feel...

- in awe of God's power displayed in the miraculous conversion of Saul.
- convicted by Saul's quick and full repentance.

Understand...

- that in contrast to Philip's efforts to spread the gospel out from Jerusalem, Saul was set on capturing Christians and bringing them back to Jerusalem.
- that Saul's spiritual eyes were opened when Jesus appeared to him, even though the light blinded him physically.
- that after believing, Saul was immediately "all in" and was baptized and received the Holy Spirit.
- that Saul was rejected in Damascus when he started preaching the gospel there, foreshadowing how much of his ministry would go.
- that Saul went back to Jerusalem and found peace with the apostles.
- that the Christians enjoyed peace now that Saul wasn't persecuting them, and the Church was edified.

Apply this understanding by...

- being quick to repent like Saul was.
- realizing that obedience to your call is the most important thing, *not* being a big shot; faithful believers like Ananias and Barnabas were just as important to the spread of Christianity as front men like Saul would later become.

now a believer and jumped in the deep end right away as an evangelist. He went from persecuting Christian evangelists to being the one who was persecuted. Philip was well-received in Samaria when he first arrived with the gospel, and many believed (Acts 8:4-8), but Saul was rejected in Damascus when he began preaching the gospel. This foreshadowed how much of Paul's mission work would go; it would often be difficult, and he would suffer (Acts 9:16), but God had many great things in store for him.

This part of the story ends with Saul back in Jerusalem, at peace with the apostles (Acts 9:28), but at odds with the unbelieving Hellenistic Jews who wanted to kill him. Contrast this with where he started in Jerusalem at the beginning of Acts 8: he was going from house to house in Jerusalem, imprisoning believers. Saul was the kind of person who went house to house; at one time he did it out of hostility, but from now on he would go about in peace.

The Church edified
Stephen's martyrdom began the spread of Christianity throughout Judea, Samaria, and Galilee as the Christians in Jerusalem were scattered. But early on, an ominous cloud hung over the scattered believers. Were persecutors like Saul going to stop the spread of Christianity? No, but it wasn't by the "victory" of the Christians that Christianity would spread; it was by the power of God turning Saul's heart to Him even while Saul was an enemy of the gospel. As a result, "the churches throughout all Judea, Galilee, and Samaria had peace and were edified. And walking in the fear of the Lord and in the comfort of the Holy Spirit, they were multiplied" (Acts 9:31).

APPLICATION

The story of Saul is striking; as soon as he heard the gospel and believed, he put all his energy into obedience. He was called by God to be the apostle to the Gentiles and immediately began working faithfully toward that calling. In other words, he was quick to repent. Jesus works game changers into our lives, major roadblocks that are supposed to change the course of our lives. But so often we treat them like speed bumps; we climb right over and keep on going. Saul's is an example of the kind of repentance that pleases the Father.

Of course, not all of us are called to be Saul, the front man. Without obedient servants like Ananias and Barnabas who were willing to advocate for Saul, he might never have attained the approval of the apostles. Their service was no less valuable than Saul's, though the outward fruit of Saul's ministry would be much greater than theirs over time.

ACTIVITIES

1. Compare and Contrast. Using Acts 8 and 9 (Lessons 6.4 and 6.5), compare and contrast Saul with the Ethiopian eunuch.

Saul	Ethiopian Eunuch

What lessons can you take away from this comparison? Be prepared to discuss your answer in class.

_____
_____
_____
_____
_____
_____
_____
_____

2. Journal Time: Repentance. Think of a time God attempted to give you a course correction, but you simply treated it as a speed bump. Pray and ask the Lord to tell you an area in your life (even a small area) where you need to repent. Write about this in the space below.

_____
_____
_____
_____
_____
_____
_____
_____
_____
_____
_____
_____

Lesson 6.5

EVALUATION

1. What was Saul doing while Philip was seeking to spread the gospel out from Jerusalem? _____
_____
_____

2. What happened to Saul when he met Jesus on the road to Damascus? _____
_____
_____

3. How did Saul behave after his conversion? _____
_____

4. How effective was Saul's first evangelism attempt in Damascus? _____
_____

5. What happened to the Church after Saul's conversion? _____
_____

LESSON 6.6

The Conversion of Cornelius

UNIT 6

THE STORY

Lesson Theme - The gospel went to the Gentiles.
At the beginning of Acts, the disciples received the Holy Spirit and many came to the Lord. Initially, however, all of the converts to Christianity were Jews or proselytes. No one really understood that the gospel was going to go to the Gentiles. Presumably, the apostles believed that Gentiles would become Christians the way they had always come to the Lord: by becoming Jews first. This would have put them in obligation to the Law *as Jews*.

But as Peter headed out on a missionary journey through the land of Israel, God spoke to him in a vision and told him that Gentiles were no longer to be considered unclean; they didn't have to submit to the Law to receive the Holy Spirit. This distinguished Christianity from every other Jewish sect and provided the basis for the expansion of Christianity throughout the world as Jesus had commanded in Acts 1.

Peter's missionary journey
Peter had preached on Pentecost and many had come to know the Lord. He was responsible for the official launch of the Church. After that, he stayed in Jerusalem until shortly after Stephen was martyred and the Church was scattered. In Acts 8:14-24, Peter and John went to Samaria where Philip had preached the gospel and many had come to the Lord. Peter then returned to Jerusalem. This next section of Acts (9:31-11:18) records Peter's first real missionary journey since Jesus ascended. Peter was taking seriously Jesus' call to bring the gospel to the ends of the earth.

OVERVIEW

The gospel had gone out to Judea and Samaria in fulfillment of Jesus' commission in Acts 1:8, but in this lesson we see a new move of the Spirit. With clear confirmation and direction from the Lord, Peter and Cornelius, a Gentile, met together. Peter preached the gospel to Cornelius and his friends and family, and before he was finished speaking, these Gentiles received the Holy Spirit—without even getting circumcised or following the Old Testament Law. This was the beginning of the mission of the Church to the *entire* world.

SOURCE MATERIAL

- Acts 9:32-11

Acts records that he travelled from Lydda to Joppa and on up to Caesarea—a fairly short trip by most standards—but it also says that he travelled through all parts of the country (Acts 9:32).

The first story recorded about Peter's missionary travels occurs in Lydda (Acts 9:32). There was already a Christian community in Lydda by the time Peter arrived. Peter found a man named Aeneas (probably a Christian) who was paralyzed and had been bedridden for eight years, and Peter said to him, "Arise and make your bed," healing the man (Acts 9:34). Word of the healing spread quickly, and many in the surrounding area turned to the Lord (Acts 9:35). So far so good—Peter was imitating Christ and spreading the gospel in the land of Judea.

45

Unit 6: The Church is Born

OBJECTIVES

Feel...

- a bit surprised that the meeting between Peter and Cornelius took *so much* confirmation from the Lord.
- excited to see how the Lord was leading the Church; it wasn't Peter's idea to bring the gospel to the Gentiles, it was God's.
- thankful that God values the ordinary faithfulness of ordinary Christians like Tabitha.

Understand...

- that the exclusive nature of Old Testament Judaism lacked what was needed to see the gospel transform the world, even with Jesus added to it.
- the basic movements of Peter's first missionary journey—to Lydda, then to Joppa and on to Caesarea.
- that Peter raised Tabitha from the dead which caused many to come to the Lord.
- how clearly the Lord directed and confirmed Cornelius' and Peter's meeting.
- that Cornelius was already a believer in God, but before hearing from Peter, he and his family had not received the Holy Spirit.
- that the Church accepted the conversion of these Gentiles as a new move of God on account of God's clear confirmation and Peter's testimony.

Apply this understanding by...

- living a life that manifests the truth that the gospel is for everyone.
- valuing ordinary faithfulness as God did with Tabitha.

Word reached Joppa, a town on the coast not far from Lydda, that Peter was in the area. There was, as in Lydda, already a Christian community in Joppa. Tabitha, a respected disciple in Joppa, had died (Acts 9:37). But the Christian community there did not lose hope; after all, Jesus had risen from the dead, why not Tabitha? So they sent for Peter. Peter came immediately and raised her from the dead. Like in Lydda, many turned to the Lord when this happened (Acts 9:42).

Tabitha was, in many ways, an ordinary Christian; she was a faithful disciple, but God raised her from the dead. This demonstrates the value God places on ordinary faithfulness. Tabitha had a very specific calling—making clothes for widows—and she did it faithfully.

Cornelius

Peter stayed in Joppa for many days at the home of a tanner named Simon (Acts 9:43). Notice that Luke draws particular attention to Simon's occupation as a tanner. Simon worked with dead animals and thus would have been perpetually unclean in regard to the Law. Luke also draws attention to Tabitha's name (Dorcas in Greek) which means gazelle (an unclean animal under Old Testament Law). Symbolically, Luke is pointing to Peter's next task: bringing the gospel to the Gentiles, who were also unclean according to the Law.

Cornelius was a faithful Gentile (a Greek). He is described as being "a devout man and one who feared God with all his household, who gave alms generously to the people, and prayed to God always" (Acts 10:2). He was a Gentile who was known as a God-fearer—that is, someone who would attend synagogue to hear the word, someone who believed in God and faithfully followed Him, but was neither a Jew nor a proselyte.

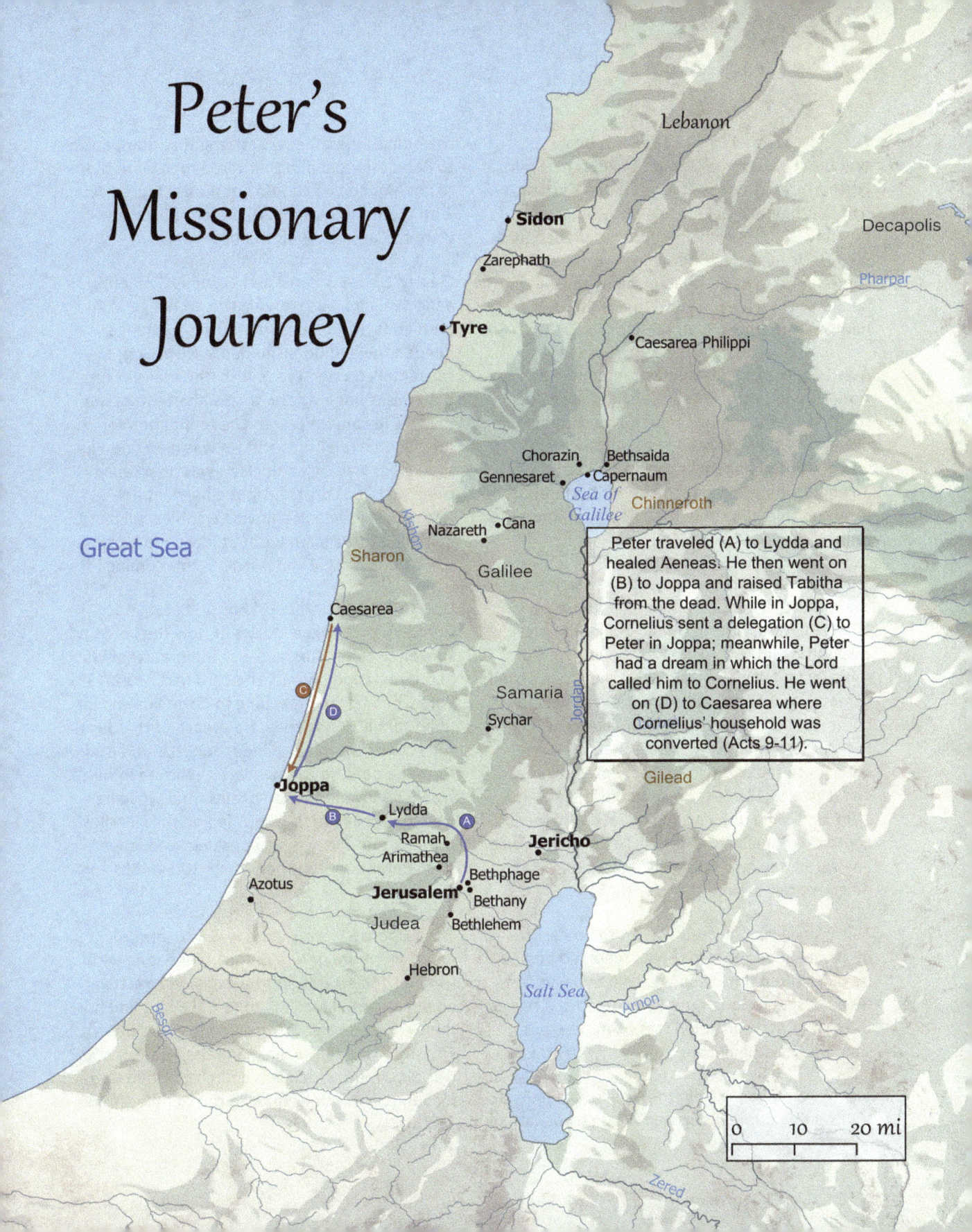

Unit 6: The Church is Born

Therefore, Cornelius was already a heaven-bound believer in God when Peter met him. Furthermore, there is indication that Cornelius had heard of and believed in Jesus; he had possibly even seen and heard Jesus preach (Acts 10:37). Nevertheless, Cornelius was missing something. He had a relationship with God, but he didn't yet have the gift of the Holy Spirit and baptism into the body of Christ.

Acts 10 records a miraculous communication from God to both Cornelius *and* Peter as God sought to bring them together. This communication from God points to the significance of what was about to happen. Cornelius was visited by an angel who commended him for his faithfulness and told him to send for Peter at Simon the tanner's house (Acts 10:4-6).

The next day, Peter had a symbolic vision on the rooftop of Simon the tanner's house (Acts 10:9-16). It was approaching noon, and Peter was getting hungry. As he was praying on the rooftop, he fell into a trance. He saw in his vision something like a sheet held together by its four corners, filled with unclean animals according to the Old Testament Law. As the sheet descended, a voice spoke, saying, "Rise, Peter; kill and eat" (Acts 10:13). Peter responded by saying, "Not so, Lord! For I have never eaten anything common or unclean" (Acts 10:14). And the voice answered, saying, "What God has cleansed you must not call common" (Acts 10:15).

This vision was repeated two more times. This might seem odd; but for Peter, who had denied the Lord three times and was told by Jesus to feed His sheep three times, the repetition served to confirm that the vision was from God and validated it as significant.

Just as Peter awoke from the trance, the delegation sent by Cornelius arrived at the front gate of the house where he was staying. The Spirit spoke to Peter and told him that three men were there to get him and he should not doubt, but go along with them (Acts 10:19-20). Peter obeyed and went to Caesarea with them.

Clearly, God saw Peter and Cornelius' meeting as a big deal and was working the exchange from both ends. More importantly, this exchange needed the additional guidance from God, because to Peter and the Jewish Christians in general, this change was *huge*. God had established the Old Testament Law as the foundation for Jew/Gentile relations, and He was now undoing that; what was called unclean was now called clean. God was destroying the barrier between Jew and Gentile and allowing Gentiles full participation in the Church without having to become Jews. Peter simply had not seen this coming.

Upon arrival at Cornelius' house, Peter and Cornelius exchanged stories of how the Lord had spoken to them, further verifying that what was about to happen was of the Lord (Acts 10:27-33). Peter then began preaching to Cornelius and all of his family and friends. He preached that Jesus, the Lord of all, was crucified, buried and raised from the dead so that *whoever* believed in Him would receive remission of sins. And while he was still speaking, the Spirit fell on the Gentiles present, and they began speaking in tongues. Then Peter baptized them (Acts 10:34-48).

The Church caught up with the Spirit
The response in Jerusalem was as expected; Peter was more or less rebuked for eating with Gentiles (Acts 11:3). But he explained exactly what happened leading up to the event and how the Gentiles so clearly received the Holy Spirit. The story was compelling, and the apostles and disciples in the Jerusalem church glorified God for sending the Holy Spirit to the Gentiles (Acts 11:18).

Lesson 6.6

APPLICATION

The gospel is for everyone. Peter had been a Jew's Jew from the day he was born. He was faithful to the Law, which, to give the guy credit, had been given to the nation of Israel by God. But God was truly doing something new during the early expansion of the Church. There were now *no* religious barriers between anyone and God. The gospel is for everyone... *for God so loved the world.*

The lesson that Peter learned in Acts 10-11 applies to all of us. Of course, it is easy to agree *theologically* that the gospel is for everyone. But let's take it a step further; Jesus loved the world by dying for it. We are called to love our neighbors by dying for them. God has put people in everyone's path who are difficult to love. It may be because of race, class or personality. In each of our lives there is someone whom we would rather not see and certainly not go out of our way to love. The gospel is for everyone, and therefore, we should love those who are the hardest to love.

A second application comes from the story of Peter raising Tabitha. God honors ordinary faithfulness. You don't have to be an apostle to be faithful in the calling God has for your life. God does not despise faithfulness.

ACTIVITIES

1. Your Purity Standards. Think of a time when you encountered someone whom you found difficult to love or who made you feel uncomfortable by being "unclean" in some way, just like Peter felt towards Cornelius. Then answer the following questions.

What was your initial reaction when you encountered the person or people?_____
_____
_____

You may have pushed through it and done the right thing, but was there any desire to keep your distance or turn away? Explain._____
_____
_____

Did you have a chance to make conversation with anyone? Was it difficult? How and why?_____
_____
_____
_____

Unit 6: The Church is Born

Did you experience any compassion for the other person or people? What did your compassion drive you to do? Did you do it? Why or why not?_____
_____
_____
_____

Would you want to spend more time with that person or those people? Why or why not?_____
_____
_____
_____

What did you learn about your own standards of cleanness?_____
_____
_____
_____

2. Study the Story. List the barriers for Peter to meet, share the gospel and eat with Cornelius and how God clearly overcame them._____
_____
_____
_____
_____
_____
_____
_____
_____
_____
_____
_____

Lesson 6.6

EVALUATION

1. In what way did an understanding of Christianity as a "second story" built onto the Old Testament Law lack when it came to evangelizing? _____
_____
_____
_____

2. Where did Peter go on his first missionary journey? _____
_____
_____

3. What happened after Peter raised Tabitha from the dead? _____
_____
_____

4. What all did the Lord do to bring Peter and Cornelius together? _____
_____
_____
_____

5. What was Cornelius' spiritual condition before he heard the gospel from Peter? _____
_____
_____

6. How was Peter's news about Cornelius received when he got back to Jerusalem? _____
_____
_____
_____

LESSON 6.7

Peter's Imprisonment

THE STORY

Lesson Theme - Peter's imprisonment as a death and resurrection story
This same Peter who once rebuked Jesus for saying that He was going to go to Jerusalem to die now was willing to face death himself in order to spread the good news of Jesus Christ. One day, of course, Peter would face martyrdom. This lesson foreshadows that calling, and his imprisonment and release are a picture of death and resurrection.

Peter and Herod
Stephen's persecution had happened at the hands of the Jewish leadership *in Jerusalem* as had the early imprisonment of Peter and John. The persecution recorded in Acts 12 happened at the hands of Roman authorities (Herod was the ruler of Israel under the authority of Rome), and foreshadows the persecution coming to Paul at the hands of Roman authorities.

Everything in this story reflects that Herod was a self-seeking despot who desired to be thought of as a god. He wanted the respect of the people, and he thought he could get it by persecuting the Christians. After he saw that killing James pleased the Jews, he set out to kill some more Christians. James had been the leader of the church in Jerusalem; the only Christian with more name-recognition than James was probably Peter, so Herod went after him (Acts 12:1-3).

Herod arrested Peter and had him thrown in prison. He didn't kill him right away because he wanted to put him on public trial after Passover (Acts 12:4). He wanted to do to Peter what he

OVERVIEW

Herod decided that it might be politically expedient to start persecuting the Church. He had James killed and it played well, so he arrested Peter next. Instead of killing Peter right away, Herod put him in prison so he could kill him on Passover. While in prison, Peter was miraculously delivered. The way the story is told, Peter experienced a sort of death and resurrection; then the Lord struck Herod dead.

SOURCE MATERIAL

- Acts 12

had done to Jesus—public trial and murder on the same day. Peter is a picture of Jesus in this story.

Peter's time in prison is pictured as a death; he was sleeping, bound between two soldiers, while more stood watch outside (Acts 12:6). Then an angel of the Lord appeared to him, struck Peter on the side and "raised him up" (Acts 12:7). Like Jesus, he was struck on the side and rose "from the dead."

The angel led Peter into the city; the gate opened on its own, and Peter and the angel entered the city (Acts 12:10). Peter had thought he was dreaming this entire time, but as soon as the angel departed, he realized what had happened. The Lord had rescued him from Herod in order to frustrate the hopes of the Jewish leaders.

Unit 6: The Church is Born

OBJECTIVES

Feel...

- sad for the persecution that the Church endured at the hands of Herod.
- excited that God delivered Peter.

Understand...

- that Herod was self-absorbed and killed James to get people to like him more.
- that Herod arrested Peter for the same reason as he had James.
- how Peter's time in prison reflected Jesus' death and resurrection.
    - Herod wanted Peter to have a public trial after Passover.
    - Peter's time in prison was like his death.
    - Peter was "struck on the side" and then "rose up" (which was his resurrection).
    - The first person Peter encountered after his resurrection was a woman.
    - The disciples didn't believe the woman's testimony.
    - Peter's guards were cross-examined by the authorities.
- that God struck Herod dead on account of his self-exaltation.

Apply this understanding by...

- walking in the footsteps of Christ, like Peter and James, whether in life or in death.

Peter went straight to the house of Mary, the mother of John, where many disciples had gathered to pray (Acts 12:12). Like Jesus had after His resurrection, the first person Peter encountered was a woman (Rhoda). The disciples didn't believe that she had actually seen Peter, just as the disciples didn't believe the women who testified to Jesus' resurrection. The disciples finally believed when they let Peter into the house.

Finally, just like after Jesus' resurrection, the ones who were supposed to be guarding were cross-examined by the authorities (Acts 12:19). While Herod executed Peter's guards since he had no use for them, Jesus' guards weren't killed because they could be used to falsely report that Jesus' body had been stolen.

At the beginning of Acts 12, Herod had James killed, but by the end of the chapter, it all came back around, and God killed Herod—"'Vengeance is Mine,' says the Lord" (Rom 12:19). Interestingly, Herod's death occurred when he dressed in his finest to give a great kingly speech. Just like Jesus had been led to His death wearing royal robes and a crown on His head, so Herod died under similar circumstances—while the people called him a god. Only Herod didn't rise from the dead. He was eaten by worms even while he was alive, and remains in his grave to this day.

Herod's death marks the end of Peter's front role in the book of Acts. Meanwhile, God called Paul to take the gospel to the Gentiles. Herod was just the first of many political rulers the gospel would confront. The gospel was going to change the world, and the first place it would change was the Roman Empire.

Lesson 6.7

APPLICATION

We are to live lives that reflect the structure of Jesus' life. This is a tough lesson to learn in our age, but it is something that comes up over and over in Acts. Stephen's death was like Jesus'. Philip, Peter and Paul all went on missionary journeys that followed the pattern of Jesus' ministry. And in this lesson, Peter was imprisoned and escaped in a way that reflects Jesus' death and resurrection. This is not just a literary nicety; we are to live lives that reflect Jesus' life just like the apostles did.

ACTIVITIES

1. Parallel Pictures. This activity is to help you see how Peter's time in prison reflected Jesus' death and resurrection. On the left side below, draw small pictures of Jesus' trial, death, and resurrection. On the right side, corresponding to each of Jesus' pictures, draw pictures of Peter's time in prison (Acts 12).

Unit 6: The Church is Born

2. Lives that Reflect Jesus. Several different times in Acts we see characters whose lives reflected Jesus' life. God wants your life to be patterned after Jesus' life too. Answer the following questions to help you figure out what it might look like to reflect Jesus' life at your age and in our culture.

What is something you could do everyday that would make your life more like Jesus' life? _____
_____
_____
_____
_____

What can you do in conversations with friends that would make your life more like Jesus' life? _____
_____
_____
_____
_____

What can you do at home and with your family to make your life look more like Jesus' life? _____
_____
_____
_____
_____

What is something you can do this week to love someone sacrificially like Jesus loves us? Make this something specific and measurable. It can be something simple, but it should cost you something—whether it's time, resources, money, your image, etc. _____
_____
_____
_____
_____
_____
_____

Lesson 6.7

EVALUATION

1. What was Herod's motivation for killing James and arresting Peter? _____

2. What was Peter's imprisonment and release from prison a metaphor for? _____

3. In what ways was Peter's experience of imprisonment like Jesus' death? _____

4. In what ways was Peter's release from prison like Jesus' resurrection? _____

5. What happened to Herod after Peter was delivered? _____

UNIT 7: THE CHURCH EXPANDS

Peter's deliverance from prison and the death of Herod end the story of the growth of the Judean church in Acts, and Paul moves center stage for the Gentile expansion of Christianity. Paul and Barnabas were sent out by their home church in Antioch to bring the gospel to the Gentiles. Wherever they went, the gospel was well-received but also drew heavy fire from the enemy.

When Paul and Barnabas returned from their successful first missionary journey, their celebration quickly turned into contention when a group of Christian legalists arrived from Jerusalem wanting to require that Gentile converts follow the Law in order to be saved. Although Paul and the leadership at Antioch knew these men were wrong, they sent a delegation to Jerusalem to settle the issue once and for all.

After returning to Antioch, Paul and Barnabas made plans to visit all the churches they had ministered in on their first missionary journey. But they strongly disagreed on whether or not to take John Mark with them. Their disagreement was so strong that they finally went in different directions. Their split ended up working out for good because it allowed Paul to cover new ground. Wherever he went, people were eager to receive the gospel, but they encountered opposition as well.

After a stop in Jerusalem and some time in his home base, Antioch, Paul set out on his third missionary journey in order to encourage the disciples. He passed through Galatia and then came to Ephesus where he stayed for two years, training disciples in the school of Tyrannus. At the end of his time in Ephesus a great riot broke out in the city because Christianity was (rightly) perceived as a threat to the idol-making business. Following the turmoil in Ephesus, Paul went through Macedonia and Greece and then set his face toward Jerusalem.

Paul was the new Jesus. He was arrested in Jerusalem and tried before the Sanhedrin, the local Roman authorities and Herod. But he didn't die in Jerusalem. He was taken to Rome where he was put under house arrest. The book of Acts never tells us the end of Paul's story—to this day, the Church continues the story from where he left off.

LESSON 7.1

Paul's First Missionary Journey

UNIT 7

THE STORY

Lesson Theme - The gospel went to the Gentiles. Before Jesus ascended, He told His disciples that they would be "witnesses to Me in Jerusalem, and in all Judea and Samaria, and to the end of the earth" (Acts 1:8). Persecution brought the first wave of missionaries out of Jerusalem and into Judea and Samaria; both Philip and Peter had journeyed through these areas. But in order for the gospel to go out to the rest of the world with any power, a significant change needed to occur; *the gospel needed to go to the Gentiles without them having to become Jews.* That's what the story of Peter and Cornelius was all about. Now the gospel could go to the Gentiles, and Paul was the one whom God had chosen for this task (Acts 9:15).

Paul and Barnabas' first missionary journey
Missionary journeys figure significantly in the spread of the gospel in Acts. So far, Philip and Peter had been on local missionary journeys (not to mention Jesus' missionary journeys around Galilee, Samaria and Judea). Paul's story recorded in the rest of the book of Acts took place in three missionary journeys and a final journey to Rome. The first missionary journey was relatively short compared to the second and third. The final journey to Rome was especially significant because the Christians were out to *convert the nations*, and the first nation they were to convert was Rome. Paul's journey to Rome represented the seed of the gospel being planted there.

OVERVIEW

Peter's deliverance from prison and the death of Herod end the story of the growth of the Judean church in Acts, and Paul moves center stage for the Gentile expansion of Christianity. Paul and Barnabas were sent out by their home church in Antioch to bring the gospel to the Gentiles. Wherever they went, the gospel was well-received but also drew heavy fire from the enemy.

SOURCE MATERIAL

Acts 13-14

Paul was the first among the missionaries to the Gentiles, but he certainly wasn't the only one. There were undoubtedly many other missionaries going out to the Gentiles beginning around this time. But Paul serves as an archetype of what missions looked like in the first century.

The beginning of Acts 13 has a lesson about how God speaks. Antioch was a powerhouse church with many respectable prophets and teachers (Acts 13:1). This made Antioch a very useful homebase for Paul in his missionary journeys. Paul knew he was called to be a missionary to the Gentiles, but God used this church to consecrate and send him (and Barnabas) out. As the church leaders were praying and fasting, the Holy Spirit spoke to them, that they were to consecrate (set apart) Paul and Barnabas and send them out as missionaries (Acts 13:2). God speaks through His Church.

Unit 7: The Church Expands

OBJECTIVES

Feel...

- attracted to the idea that a church can hear God's voice through the Holy Spirit.
- excited that the gospel was going to the Gentiles.
- amazed at the polarizing reaction to the gospel among the Gentiles.

Understand...

- that Herod's death marks a shift from a story about Peter and Israel to Paul and the Gentile world hearing the gospel.
- that God used the church in Antioch to speak to Paul and Barnabas.
- that Paul and Barnabas still had a lot to learn even though God called them to the mission field.
- that the gospel sent shock waves through the Gentile cities Paul and Barnabas visited.
- that the gospel offers the possibility of a meaningful life *even in the here and now*.
- that the change of Saul's name to Paul (meaning humble) contrasts nicely with Bar-Jesus' self-glorifying name change.
- that both in Pisidian Antioch and Iconium many believed, but the cities still turned against Paul and Barnabas.
- that miracles set the stage for Paul and Barnabas' gospel ministry in most of the places they went.

Apply this understanding by...

- seeking to hear God's voice spoken through God's people.

In any missionary endeavor, there is a learning curve. Questions such as how the gospel will be received or what particular challenges the gospel will face in *this* culture with *this* religion are often unknowns until experimented with on the mission field. This was *especially* true of Paul and Barnabas. Let's face it, they didn't really know what they were doing when they set out. They teach us an important lesson: just because you are called to a particular mission doesn't make it automatic; there is a learning curve, but you still need to be diligent in the task God has given you.

What Paul and Barnabas found was that the gospel was a bolt of lightning in Roman culture. It tapped into an intense hunger people had, and it created an immediate and vast following, while at the same time turning the Roman world upside down. This was all complicated by the fact that in every city Paul and Barnabas went, there was already a Jewish community, some of whom were ripe for the gospel and some who reacted just like the Jewish leadership in Jerusalem had. Furthermore, every synagogue also had a number of Gentile attendees, people who believed in the God of the Jews but didn't want to become Jews and take on a Jewish lifestyle to become part of Israel. These Gentiles would have been particularly attracted to the gospel because it provided a way to get to God (through Jesus Christ) without having to meet the requirements of the Law (circumcision, dietary laws, clothing laws, purity laws, etc.).

We mentioned above that the gospel turned the Roman world upside down. To understand what the good news of Jesus Christ would mean in that context, we need to understand the Roman culture a little bit better. In America, we like to think about politics, religion and our social relationships as separate areas of life. In Rome, politics and religion were two facets of the same thing; religious life and political life were one and the same. For Greeks who believed in the gods, life was not completely random; the gods actually controlled life in many ways, but it was still chaotic. Everything happened at the whim of whatever god happened to be in control. There really was no hope for the future. Likewise, politics offered no hope for the same reason.

Furthermore, life was really hard; disease was rampant, and except for the very rich, life in the city was lived in incredibly tight quarters with unsanitary conditions. Life was lived meal to meal, and work was hard. The gospel offered something worth living for and an ultimate hope—one day the wrongs of others, society, the government and any personal enemies would be made right by Jesus Christ. Not only that, the gospel also offered a way of being together as community—an ethic of neighbor-love that was virtually non-existent in that society. The gospel offered hope, not just in the resurrection, but that life could be better right now by building a certain kind of community where life was shared in a meaningful way. In short, the gospel offered the possibility of the kingdom in the here and now.

Paul and Barnabas came first to the Island of Cyprus (Acts 13:4). As they worked their way across the island, they preached in the synagogues first wherever they went. There was a theological reason for this: the Jews were God's people and the gospel was to go to them first. But there was also a practical reason: the synagogue included a number of God-fearers (Gentiles who already believed in God), and both the Jews and the Gentiles in the synagogue were likely to be more receptive to the gospel than those who believed in the pagan gods of the Romans.

When Paul and Barnabas came to Paphos, they found that the proconsul (the head of the province—something like what we call a governor) was receptive to the gospel, but a sorcerer and false-prophet known as Bar-Jesus was trying to dissuade him from believing (Acts 13:6-8). Bar-Jesus was not likely the sorcerer's real name; rather, in all likelihood, he had taken on the name to associate himself with Jesus Christ, as though he was personally connected to that reputable miracle-worker. His name indicates that he was trying to make big claims about himself to secure his reputation. Saul, for the first time, is called Paul here. While Saul is a Jewish name, Paul is a Greek name, so it was better for his mission work in Greek lands. Paul means "small" or "humble" and provides a nice contrast to the claim Bar-Jesus was making for himself. While Bar-Jesus was claiming to be a Jesus-figure, Paul was just a small and humble follower of Jesus.

But when Paul rebuked Bar-Jesus in the power of the Holy Spirit and caused him to go blind (Acts 13:9-11), he filled the role that Jesus did when he (then Saul) was converted. Paul, in his humility, was more like Jesus than Bar-Jesus was in his arrogance and self-exaltation.

From Paphos, Paul and Barnabas went to Pisidian Antioch (Acts 13:14). As was their custom, they went first into the synagogue and preached the gospel there. The interest in the gospel was astonishing. Not only were Jews, proselytes and God-fearers attracted to the gospel, the next Sabbath, nearly the whole city gathered to hear the word (Acts 13:44). But the Jewish leaders were jealous (like in Jerusalem) and started to oppose Paul and Barnabas. Paul and Barnabas pushed back against the opposition with great boldness, and many believed. But ultimately, the Jewish leaders were successful in turning the people against them, and Paul and Barnabas shook the dust off their feet as they left the city (Acts 13:51). They were following in the footsteps of the Messiah who taught His disciples to shake the dust off their feet if they were rejected in a city.

Paul and Barnabas went on to Iconium where a similar conflict occurred. While many believed, the Jews turned many Gentiles against them. Paul and Barnabas pushed back hard against the opposition; they remained there a long time, performing many miracles. Ultimately, however, the city was divided and there was a plot to kill them, so they left (Acts 14:1-7).

From Iconium, they went to Lystra where Paul healed a crippled man (Acts 14:8-10). When the Gentiles saw what Paul had done, they thought Paul and Barnabas were gods! They called Barnabas Zeus and Paul Hermes and were preparing to offer sacrifices to them. All of this was happening in the local language, so Paul and Barnabas didn't realize at first what was going on. When they learned what the people were thinking, they argued against it and were barely able to dissuade the crowd from sacrificing to them. Clearly, their time in Lystra turned out to be an unsuccessful missionary endeavor.

The people who had opposed them in Pisidian Antioch and Iconium caught up with them and convinced the crowd to join them in opposing Paul and Barnabas. They stoned Paul and left him for dead outside the city (Acts 14:19). The disciples gathered around him, and he ended up being fine (miracle perhaps?). He went directly back into the city that stoned him and left the next day for Derbe where they also won many disciples. Paul and Barnabas returned through the cities they had visited to encourage the saints and appoint elders before finally heading back to Antioch. When they got back, they told the church there what the Lord had done among the Gentiles, and they remained in Antioch a long time (Acts 14:27-28).

APPLICATION

Paul and Barnabas were called to the mission field when the Holy Spirit spoke to leaders in the church at Antioch. God loves to speak to us and often will as we individually listen to His voice, but He also loves to use the Church to speak to His people. It is especially important to listen to what God is saying through His people on major decisions. This is *not* just listening to the wisdom of God's people as they hear your situation and give advice. That's important too and certainly a part of hearing from the Lord, but it also requires cultivating relationships with people who actually hear from the Lord and will give you counsel on that basis.

Lesson 7.1

ACTIVITIES

1. Map It. Mark and label Paul's first missionary journey on the blank map at the beginning of this lesson. Use the information in Acts 13-14 to construct your map.

2. Roman Culture Research. Research one of the following aspects of Roman culture.
- Roman religion
- Roman politics
- Roman economics
- Living conditions/standard of living for the average Roman citizen

Use the space below to record your findings, noting the ways Roman culture differed from our culture.

Unit 7: The Church Expands

Based on your findings, how might the gospel of Jesus Christ have been appealing to the Romans?

Lesson 7.1

EVALUATION

1. Who is the central character in the book of Acts up to chapter 13? _____

2. After Herod's death, who becomes the central character in Acts? Why? _____
_____
_____
_____

3. How did God speak to Paul and Barnabas in order to get them to go on their first missionary journey? _____
_____

4. How were Paul and Barnabas received on their first missionary journey? _____
_____
_____

5. What did the gospel offer that was appealing to Gentile unbelievers? _____
_____
_____

6. What does the name "Paul" mean? _____

    What does "Bar-Jesus" mean? _____

    Explain the irony in these names. _____
_____

7. What kind of ministry did Paul and Barnabas engage in wherever they went? _____
_____
_____

LESSON 7.2

The Jerusalem Council

UNIT 7

THE STORY

Lesson Theme - The first Church conflict: leadership and controversy in the Church

Peter and Paul both learned from first-hand experience that God had accepted Gentiles into the Church without requiring them to be circumcised or keep the Old Testament Law. This came as a surprise to the apostles. They certainly expected the gospel to go to the Gentiles, but they probably expected that in order to be saved, Gentiles would have to be circumcised and become Jews. We saw Peter's surprise when God told him Gentiles were now clean and directed him to preach the gospel to Cornelius and his family (Acts 10-11). When Peter brought word back to Jerusalem, the believers there initially objected, but after Peter told them the story, they glorified God.

By Acts 15, it was well known among the apostles and leaders of the Church that God had accepted the Gentiles into the Church—*as Gentiles*. However, there remained a large sect of Christians, many of them converted Pharisees, who didn't believe that Gentiles could get in that easily. They believed that to be accepted by God, Gentiles would need to be circumcised and obey the Mosaic Law (these people became known as *Judaizers*). Of course, the issue had been settled among the apostles in Jerusalem, but as these Pharisees went out to the surrounding area where the apostles weren't strongly represented, there was considerable controversy.

Finally, these men arrived in Antioch, where Paul and Barnabas had just returned from their

OVERVIEW

When Paul and Barnabas returned from their first missionary journey they were jazzed, but their celebration was quickly turned into contention when a group of Christian legalists arrived from Jerusalem. They were teaching that it was necessary to require Gentile converts to be circumcised and keep the Law of Moses in order to be saved, which obviously Paul and Barnabas had not done on their recent mission trip. The church at Antioch sent a delegation to Jerusalem to meet with the apostles and elders to get some resolution on the issue. When they arrived in Jerusalem and met with the leaders and their contenders, there was an intense disagreement. Eventually, Peter spoke and said that clearly the Lord was accepting the Gentiles without requiring them to keep the Law and so should everyone else. Paul backed Peter up with his experiences on the mission field, and James made an exegetical case from the Old Testament, proving that this was God's plan all along. The leadership sent a letter with Paul back to Antioch to settle the issue among the Gentiles.

SOURCE MATERIAL

- Acts 15:1-35
- Proverbs 18:17

missionary journey to the Gentiles, and the inevitable conflict ensued. Paul and Barnabas "had no small dissension" (Acts 15:2) with these men.

69

Unit 7: The Church Expands

OBJECTIVES

Feel...

- Paul and Barnabas' frustration at hearing the legalists after returning from their first missionary journey.
- impressed by the unity that provided the basis to have the doctrinal contention.
- thankful for the careful leadership of Peter, Paul and James and how they firmly decided the case without causing a major split in the Church.

Understand...

- the background and content of the theological contention in Acts 15.
- that Acts 15 records a great dispute before an official counsel of the apostles and elders.
- Peter's case—that God had decided the Gentiles would be accepted by faith, just like the Jews.
- Paul and Barnabas' practical case—they had seen the Lord do great things among the Gentiles.
- James' case from Amos—God intended this all along and prefigured it in David's tabernacle.
- the purpose of the council's letter—to establish their decision as the official teaching in all the churches.

Apply this understanding by...

- properly submitting to God-given leadership in your life.
- practicing godly leadership now as the Lord gives opportunities.

Finally, the church at Antioch determined that Paul, Barnabas, and some other representatives should go to Jerusalem to settle the matter with the apostles and elders there.

It is important to imagine what this would have been like for Paul and Barnabas. They had just returned from a remarkable journey—they had performed miracles and seen many come to the Lord. They had also suffered greatly—Paul had been stoned, nearly to death, for goodness sake! And then these "religious" men from Jerusalem came and told them and the rest of the church at Antioch that the mission they had just returned from was a farce; God wasn't really accepting the Gentiles on the basis of simple faith in His Son. Obviously, the arguments of these men were *not* compelling to Paul and Barnabas... they were infuriating.

However, Paul did not exercise his apostolic authority to summarily dismiss them and continue with his ministry. He didn't just leave the Antioch church and his critics behind and start over somewhere else. Paul knew that the unity of the body and the future of the Church were at stake. This controversy really did have the potential of tearing the Church in two and doing great damage among the Gentiles if it wasn't dealt with properly. These men from Jerusalem preaching the circumcision of the Gentiles wouldn't have stopped in Antioch, but would have continued on their own missionary journey, undermining the work of Paul and Barnabas everywhere they went.

Had this controversy happened in the evangelical church in America today, Paul might have just started a new denomination. There are several lessons here about how the Church *should* behave. Antioch and Jerusalem were the two biggest church hubs at this point in time. But that didn't mean that each city had a mega-church. Churches at this early stage in the development met in multiple homes. There is no way to know exactly how many house churches there would've been in Jerusalem or Antioch, but we can make some educated guesses. We know that there were at least 3,000 believers in Jerusalem after Pentecost, but many of them would have left the city when the persecution began. For the sake of the example, let's say that as many as half of them left, leaving only 1,500 believers in Jerusalem. Homes in Jerusalem were generally small; so, as a high estimate, each house church could've held perhaps 50 people, meaning that there were about 60 house churches in the city. Something comparable was probably going on in Antioch.

But these churches were operating in unity and could be referred to as the "church at Jerusalem" or the "church at Antioch." This meant that there was some sort of defined structure and leadership in each city bringing these communities together (probably in an informal manner). These churches saw it as important to maintain unity within their local community, but they didn't stop there. When the problem arose of whether Gentiles needed to follow the Law or not, the *united* church in Antioch sent representatives to the *united* church in Jerusalem. The early Church valued both local unity *and* long distance unity. Disagreement among brethren didn't mean an occasion for some kind of a split, but a chance to come together to settle the issue as a unified Church.

The council
When Paul and the rest of the representatives from Antioch arrived in Jerusalem, we are told that they were "received by the church and the apostles and the elders" (Acts 15:4). As far as the apostolic leadership in Jerusalem was concerned, this issue had already been settled when Peter had told them of the conversion of Cornelius. As soon as Paul and the representatives arrived, they recounted the stories of what God had done among the Gentiles. This provoked a reaction from the Pharisees who had become believers; they objected and said that the Gentiles needed to be circumcised and taught to keep the Mosaic Law (Acts 15:5). And so, the official council was convened.

The meeting of this council provides a great example of how to deal with large-scale disagreement among believers. The early Church's disagreement was happening within the context of an authority structure, but there was not one man on top. The apostles and elders came together as the ruling authorities to decide the issue—it was not a free for all. Of course, we already know that the apostles and elders were in agreement that the Gentiles didn't have to follow the Mosaic Law; but nevertheless, they allowed the disagreement to play out before they presented their case. There had been "much dispute" (Acts 15:7), meaning all the contentious arguments had been laid out, before the leadership spoke up.

Appropriately, Peter was the first among the apostles and elders to speak (Acts 15:7). He had been chosen to be the first to preach the gospel among the Jews on Pentecost and the first to bring the gospel to Cornelius and his family, the first Gentiles converted. He had heard directly from God on the issue, and everyone knew it. And that was exactly the point he made, "God gave them the same Holy Spirit He gave us, and He did it without requiring them to be circumcised" (Acts 15:8-9*). But Peter was not just making an argument, he was rebuking the Judaizers: "Why do you test God by putting a yoke on the neck of the disciples which neither our fathers nor we were able to bear?" (Acts 15:10).

The last sentence of Peter's speech is really important. We would expect Peter to say, "We believe that...*they* will be saved in the same manner as *we* are." Instead, he said exactly the opposite: "We believe that through the grace of the Lord Jesus Christ *we* shall be saved in the same manner as *they*" (Acts 15:11, emphasis added). The fact that the Gentiles had received the Holy Spirit without being circumcised was a lesson for the Jews. Many of the Jews had already been circumcised and been following the Law for years. They knew they were saved by faith in Christ, but many of them thought that their faithfulness to the Law and their circumcision prequalified them. But the lesson Peter learned was that, regarding salvation, God no longer made a distinction between Jews and Gentiles—salvation and the gift of the Holy Spirit was freely available to all men by faith in Christ alone. Peter was rebuking the Pharisee Christians, but he was also preaching the good news to them: they were saved by simple faith in Christ, just like the Gentiles.

Paul and Barnabas spoke next, telling everyone about what God had already done among the Gentiles (Acts 15:12) in order to drive the point home that this was not just a theory about what God might be up to among the Gentiles. He *had* saved them by simple faith, so the Church needed to get on board.

Finally, James made a theological case from the Old Testament (Acts 15:13-21). In the Old Testament lesson on David's tabernacle (OT Lesson 8.5) we saw that something very unique was going on. In contrast to the tabernacle before David's time, *and* in contrast to worship at Solomon's temple, David's tabernacle involved Gentiles in worship (review that lesson for more information). Of course, that wasn't really a surprise; God's very first promise to Abraham was that as God's special people, Abraham's descendants would be blessed by God and in turn be a blessing to the Gentiles.

In Acts 15:15-17, James made reference to Amos 9:11-12 where Amos prophesies that David's tabernacle would be restored so that all the Gentiles could know God. James was claiming that the salvation that was happening among the Gentiles was not an anomaly. God had intended all along to restore the kind of worship, through Jesus Christ, that had gone on at David's tabernacle. The fact that this kind of worship was now happening was indication that the prophecy was being fulfilled and a great occasion to rejoice.

With that, the issue was settled. The apostles and elders sent a letter throughout the region indicating their decision. The letter was accompanied by several witnesses from both Antioch and Jerusalem (Acts 15:22-31).

It is interesting to note that the apostles and elders didn't excommunicate the Pharisees, perhaps because there were way too many of them. Instead, they just ensured that the official message was known throughout the churches, and over time the problem went away. Of course, it didn't go away without much work from Paul and the other apostles who had to contend with Judaizers everywhere they went. But they treated it as an in-house problem; these Pharisees were real Christians, they just misunderstood the nature of the gospel. This misunderstanding was a serious problem, but one that could be dealt with without anathematizing all of them, a process which would have torn the Church in two.

APPLICATION

The big lesson from this chapter comes from seeing how Paul and the leadership in Jerusalem handled their disagreement. From their perspective, the issue of *who was right* was simple; it was clear to them that God was calling Gentiles into the Church without them having to become Jews. Furthermore, the leadership had the authority to bring down the hammer, to refuse to hear any arguments about the issue and simply excommunicate the Judaizers. Rather, they didn't allow the dispute to come to a head and heard arguments from both sides.

On the other hand, when they did finally decide the issue, they left no doubt as to which side was right and which was wrong. Peter and James both firmly defended the freeness of the gospel. Furthermore, they made sure their decision was known—they sent a letter out to the churches with witnesses and all. And still, they didn't excommunicate the Judaizers.

The nature of the kind of leadership we see from the apostles and elders here is not *simple.* They displayed a prudent combination of tactical wisdom (knowing that squashing the Judaizers might provoke backlash), grace (hearing all the arguments) and firmness (deciding the case and disseminating their decision).

The application here is two-sided. We don't know how the Judaizers responded to this decision. Clearly, the fact that the apostles felt the need to send out a letter indicates that they were at least concerned that some of the Judaizers would blow off their decision and continue to spread their false message. The *right* response for the Judaizers was to both believe the gospel and accept this decision. Likewise, when we are under God-given leadership, we have a responsibility to submit—even when we don't agree with their decision. This is not an absolute rule; there are times when following God means not following your God-given leaders when they step outside of their God-given authority. Additionally, submitting to God-given authority doesn't mean that you never have disagreements. But nevertheless, submission to authority is the foundational principle.

The other side of the application is for when *you* are in a position of leadership. Don't think too narrowly here; we are leaders whenever we are around those who look up to us or whenever we are given responsibility over someone else. The first lesson here is to hear a case before making a decision, *even if* you're sure you know the whole story and how you will decide. You may still end up changing your mind, and it is unjust to decide a case without hearing both sides (see Prov 18:17). Secondly, make decisions according to what's right. Peter and the leadership knew the answer because they had heard from God—they weren't just making stuff up

Unit 7: The Church Expands

1. Journal Time: What Side Am I On? This lesson provides us with a biblical way of resolving conflict. When it comes to conflict, most of us tend towards one end of the spectrum or the other. On one end of the spectrum are those who will argue just for the sake of argument and want to win at all costs, even if it means hurting someone else. On the other end of the spectrum are those who actively avoid conflict and will even sacrifice the truth in order to keep the peace. Spend some time thinking about what side of this spectrum you tend towards. Think of a specific area of conflict in your life and pray about how you can approach this conflict from a more godly perspective. Write your thoughts and prayers in the space below.

Lesson 7.2

EVALUATION

1. How did the apostles and elders (Peter, Paul, James and others) know that God had accepted the Gentiles without them having to be circumcised and keep the Law? _____
_____
_____
_____
_____

2. When the apostles and elders called a meeting to deal with the question of *how* the Gentiles were saved, what was the first thing that happened? _____
_____

3. Peter was the first to silence the dispute and speak up; summarize what he said. _____
_____
_____

4. In what way did Paul and Barnabas make their case that God accepted the Gentiles apart from becoming Jews? _____
_____
_____

5. What did James say to make the case from the Old Testament? _____
_____
_____
_____

6. What was the purpose of the letter that the apostles and elders wrote? _____
_____
_____
_____

LESSON 7.3

Paul's Second Missionary Journey

UNIT 7

THE STORY

Lesson Theme - The gospel breaks pagan culture. The theme that comes to the forefront in this lesson is the power of the gospel to "break" Roman society. The Romans' entire social order was built on worship of demons (what they called gods). When Paul came along preaching the gospel, the gods began to lose their power; the gospel sent this pagan society into a tailspin.

Narrative overview: the second journey
After the issue of the Judaizers had been settled in Antioch, Paul and Barnabas decided that they should return to the cities they had visited on their first missionary journey to check up on them (Acts 15:36). That is the premise that drove both the second and third missionary journeys. Paul and Barnabas ended up having a disagreement over whether John Mark should come along, and they parted ways (Acts 15:37-39). Paul chose a prophet named Silas to join him on his journey instead. Paul and Barnabas were just as human as the rest of us; disagreeing is okay. In fact, in this case, it appears that Barnabas headed out toward Cyprus following the route they took on their first missionary journey (we deduce this not only from the fact that this was their original plan, but also because one of their goals was to deliver the decrees from the Jerusalem council to the churches they had been in—and we know that Paul didn't do it in most of the cities). Barnabas' work freed Paul and his team to cover a lot of new ground. In fact, Paul headed through Syria into Cilicia toward Derbe and Lystra which were among the last towns he had visited on his first missionary journey before

OVERVIEW

After returning to Antioch, Paul and Barnabas made plans to visit all the churches they had ministered in on their first missionary journey. But they strongly disagreed on whether or not to take John Mark with them. Their disagreement was so strong that they finally went in different directions. Their split ended up working out for good, allowing Barnabas to visit the churches from their previous trip and freeing Paul to cover new ground where he shared the gospel, cast out demons and saw the kingdom of God break Roman society and bring new life to the Gentiles.

SOURCE MATERIAL

- Acts 15:36-18:22

he had returned to Antioch. After that, Paul didn't visit any of the cities he had visited on his first missionary journey. Instead, with Barnabas on that detail, Paul was free to cover lots of new ground to spread the gospel. It turned out their disagreement allowed the gospel to go forth much quicker. Praise be to God.

In the region of Derbe and Lystra, Paul picked up Timothy to travel with them (Acts 16:1). From there, they headed off to the north and went through the region of Galatia, then back to the southwest through the region of Phrygia, but they were forbidden by the Holy Spirit to preach in Asia. When they came to Troas on the east coast of the Aegean, Paul had a vision in which

Unit 7: The Church Expands

OBJECTIVES

Feel...

- excitement at the power of the gospel.
- surprise at how the gospel broke pagan society.

Understand...

- Paul and Barnabas' intentions when they were preparing to head out: to visit and encourage the churches and deliver the letter from the apostles and elders.
- why Paul and Barnabas decided to go separate ways: because they strongly disagreed on whether or not John Mark should go along.
- that it ended up being better for them to go separate ways because it allowed Paul to cover new ground while Barnabas visited the churches.
- that the gospel (of Jesus Christ as King) threatened to completely undo pagan society that depended on demon/idol worship to hold things together.
- that the gospel had to break Roman society before it could build the kingdom of God there.

Apply this understanding by...

- recognizing how broken our society is.
- seeking ways to bless the lost, broken and confused in our culture.

he was called to go to Macedonia across the sea (Acts 16:9).

So they sailed across the sea and ended up in Philippi. There they met a woman named Lydia who received the gospel and was baptized along with her family (Acts 16:15). She invited them to stay at her house, which they did (c.f. Matt 10:12-13). While they were there, Paul cast a divining spirit out of a slave girl who had been making her masters a lot of money. Of course, her masters were offended, but it went a lot deeper than that. A whole multitude reacted and threw Paul and Silas in prison while they tried to drum up official charges to bring against them (Acts 16:23).

While in prison, the Lord sent an earthquake which opened all the doors and broke the chains of Paul and Silas as well as those of the other prisoners (Acts 16:26). The prison guard woke up and saw the doors open and assumed all the prisoners had escaped. He was about to kill himself (he knew he would get killed by the magistrates anyway), when Paul and those with him said, "Do yourself no harm, for we are all here!" (Acts 16:28).

In order to prevent the jailer from killing himself or being killed by his superiors, they had to remain in his custody. So they went back to his house with him (after all, what good is a jail with all the doors and chains broken). As a result, the jailer and his whole household were saved (Acts 16:33).

Paul and Silas put their lives on the line to save the jailer and his family—this is how the gospel works. We follow in the footsteps of Jesus. As a result, Paul and Silas were freed by the magistrates and left the city (Acts 16:35-36).

It is worth noting the similarities between what happened here in Philippi with what happened when Jesus freed the Gadarene demoniac in Mark 5 (see Lesson 4.3). Paul cast out a demon like Jesus cast Legion out of the demoniac. In both stories, it created an uproar and everyone wanted them to leave (Jesus in Mark 5 and Paul in Acts 16). We'll return to this below when we talk about how the message of Jesus upset the societal order.

From Philippi, Paul and his team travelled along the Macedonian coastline down through Amphipolis and Apollonia and came to Thessalonica (Acts 17:1). Paul had a very effective ministry in the synagogue for three weeks, and many came to the Lord. But the unbelieving Jews became jealous and attacked Jason's house where they thought Paul was staying. They dragged Jason and some other disciples to the city officials, accusing them of harboring a criminal. The officials took the charges seriously, but released Jason after collecting security.

Paul left the city and headed to Berea, where the Jews of the city were much more fair-minded and listened to Paul and searched the Scriptures to verify his teachings (Acts 17:11). But it didn't take long for the hostile Jews from Thessalonica to hear that Paul was in Berea, so Timothy and Silas stayed behind to disciple the new believers while Paul sailed to Athens.

Paul sent for Timothy and Silas to come to Athens and meanwhile waited there for them on his own. It was unusual for Paul to be alone like this; his normal practice was to wait for his companions to arrive before addressing the people of the city. But the idolatry of the place motivated him to reason in the synagogue and the marketplace with the Gentile philosophers (Acts 17:16-17). The Athenians were thinkers and philosophers and were interested in what Paul had to say, so they allowed him to address them in the Areopagus (this was a public court often used for philosophical discussion).

One of the Athenian altars had an inscription that said "to the unknown god" (Acts 17:23). Since Paul knew that God was unknown to them, he used this altar as a reference to the Creator God and told the story of God creating and coming to redeem the world. Some mocked him, and some believed (Acts 17:32-34).

Paul went next to Corinth, where he met met up with Timothy and Silas (Acts 18:1, 5). He worked there with Aquila and Priscilla who were tentmakers like he was and spent his Saturdays in the synagogue, reasoning with the Jews. The gospel was well-received, and they spent 18 months there, teaching the Word (Acts 18:11). The Jews sought legal recourse against them, but God protected them from all harm.

Finally, Paul headed back to Antioch, thus ending his first missionary journey. He also went down to Jerusalem during his stay at Antioch. While on his mission, he had apparently taken a Nazarite vow which he needed to fulfill, and he wanted to celebrate one of the feasts there (Acts 18:21-22).

Unit 7: The Church Expands

APPLICATION

Wherever Paul went, the gospel caused riots, confusion and anger. This was because many people knew that the gospel was a major threat to their pagan societies. We have the luxury of looking back on history and seeing that these people were exactly right—their society was threatened by the gospel, *and Christianity would ultimately dismantle and rebuild western society.*

The reason why the gospel was such a threat is pretty simple. The Roman world revolved around the worship of gods, magic and sorcery—principalities and powers of the demonic realm. And to be clear, it wasn't just religious life that revolved around these gods. The people's economic, political and social life depended on the gods. For example, when Paul cast a very profitable demon out of a slave girl, he was jailed and taken before the city officials. Why such a drastic response for such a small thing? Demon infestations were common, and there were sorcerers who cast them out all the time. The reason for the strong reaction was that first of all, Paul took away their source of income. Secondly, he cast out the demon with such ease and without resorting to sorcery—he did it in such a way that everyone knew that Jesus had cast out the demon. Paul's act undermined their sorcery.

In the next lesson we learn how something similar, though on an even larger scale, happened in Ephesus. In that city, everything was connected to the worship of the goddess Diana. The craftsmen of the city found their livelihood by making her idols; their public social space was ordered around her temple; and their political life was driven by their commitment to her. When the gospel began to spread in Ephesus, a few insightful worshipers of Diana saw where the trajectory was headed and began a riot.

This has great practical import for us. First of all, the gospel must break before it can build. The great commission was to disciple the nations, but before the nations can be disciples, the demons that hold them together must fall. In the centuries following the rise of Christianity, Roman society completely fell apart before it was rebuilt under the authority of Christ (as best they could at their place in history).

We live in a time when our society is falling apart in many ways—but in very different ways than it did in the first century. Some of the changes (homosexual marriage, for example) are being pushed on our society by those who want to destroy all remains of Christianity that still dwell in our culture. Christendom is dying... in fact, it's nearly dead. But this is not all bad, for God loves a resurrection story. Christendom 2.0 is coming and when it does, we will have lots of work to do in rebuilding a new Christian society. In the meantime, we live in a society of confused, lost, and broken people. Fighting against them won't do any good—especially if they are trying to persecute you. "Bless those who persecute you, bless and do not curse" (Rom 12:14). Broken people are generally eager to receive a blessing, even a blessing in the name of Jesus. That is our calling during this time.

Lesson 7.3

ACTIVITIES

1. Journal Time: Bless the Broken. According to Romans 12:14, we are to bless those who persecute us. By blessing others in the name of Jesus, we can be a part of rebuilding a resurrected Christianity in our world.

What are some specific and practical things you can do or say to bless others? _____
_____
_____
_____

How can you act on these ideas this week? _____
_____
_____
_____

After blessing someone, write about your experience below. _____
_____
_____
_____
_____

2. Think it Through. Paul and Barnabas had a major disagreement over whether or not they should bring John Mark on their second missionary journey. The disagreement was so acute that they ended up going separate ways. This turned out to be a good thing for the furtherance of the gospel as Barnabas was able to go back and encourage those they had visited on their first missionary journey, leaving Paul free to go on to Macedonia and preach the gospel in new cities. Nevertheless, it seems odd to us that men like Paul and Barnabas would have such a sharp disagreement. The Bible doesn't give us all the details of the disagreement, but we have enough to get an idea of what might have happened. Consider Acts 13:13, 15:36-41 and Colossians 4:10 and answer the questions below.

Why was Paul convinced that it was a bad idea to take John Mark with them? _____
_____

Unit 7: The Church Expands

What arguments do you think Paul used with Barnabas? _____
_____
_____
_____

Why do you think Barnabas was determined to take John Mark with them? _____
_____
_____

What do their differences tell you about their personalities? _____
_____
_____

What do you think was the right thing to do? _____
_____
_____

Is it okay for Christians to disagree on something like this? Were Paul and Barnabas sinning by disagreeing and going different directions? _____
_____
_____

How will seeing this disagreement teach you to think about disagreements you will inevitably see between godly people you respect in the future? _____
_____
_____

3. Map it. Mark and label Paul's second missionary journey on the blank map at the beginning of this lesson. Use the information in Acts 15:36-18:22 to construct your map.

Lesson 7.3

EVALUATION

1. What did Paul and Barnabas want to accomplish on their second missionary journey? _____
_____
_____
_____

2. Paul and Barnabas disagreed on whether to take John Mark and ended up going separate ways—was this a good or a bad thing? _____
_____
_____

3. Everywhere Paul went, the gospel caused a violent reaction from pagans. Why was this? _____
_____
_____
_____

4. Name one way the gospel threatened pagan society. _____
_____

83

LESSON 7.4

Paul's Third Missionary Journey

UNIT 7

THE STORY

Lesson Theme - The importance of disciplemaking

Paul was a committed evangelist, but, especially on his third missionary journey, Paul spent far more time discipling believers than he did preaching the gospel to pagans. Actually, discipleship was Paul's central aim throughout his ministry, and it should be ours as well.

Narrative overview: the third journey

After Paul spent some time at his home base in Antioch, he headed out again to strengthen the disciples in the cities he had visited before (Acts 18:23). He first went through Galatia and Phrygia, probably following a similar path as on his second missionary journey—through Lystra and Derbe and eventually ending up at Ephesus. He went to the synagogue and taught there for a while, but eventually moved his discipleship ministry into the school of Tyrannus (likely renting space there) for two whole years, teaching them in the way of the Lord (Acts 19:9-10).

During his time in Ephesus, the Lord enabled Paul to perform powerful miracles of healing, such that even his handkerchief could heal the sick (Acts 19:11-12)! Some itinerant Jewish exorcists saw what Paul was able to do, so they thought they would try out the name of Jesus. The seven sons of Sceva (a Jewish chief priest) were among those who tried this technique. When they did so, the demon they tried to cast out in the name of Jesus said, "Jesus I know, and Paul I know; but who are you?" (Acts 19:15). Then the man who was possessed by that spirit attacked and injured them, and they fled naked and bleeding!

Now, Paul had real power in the name of Jesus, and everyone knew it. So as word got around about the embarrassing story of the sons of Sceva being beat up by a demon-possessed man, Jesus' name was glorified all the more (Acts 19:17). Jesus was powerful enough that Paul could simply invoke His name and amazing things would happen, but His name couldn't simply be used as an incantation.

Jesus' authority completely undermined the reputation and power of sorcery in Ephesus; many sorcerers burned a huge pile of magic books

OVERVIEW

After a stop in Jerusalem and some time in his home base, Antioch, Paul set out on his third missionary journey in order to encourage the disciples. He passed through Galatia and then came to Ephesus where he stayed for two years, training disciples in the school of Tyrannus. At the end of his time in Ephesus a great riot broke out in the city against the Christians because Christianity was (rightly) perceived as a threat to the idol-making business. Following the turmoil in Ephesus, Paul went through Macedonia and Greece and then set his face toward Jerusalem.

SOURCE MATERIAL

- Acts 18:23-21:16

85

Unit 7: The Church Expands

OBJECTIVES

Feel...

- inspired by Paul's commitment to make disciples.
- convicted about the need to be discipled and make disciples.

Understand...

- that Paul spent two years teaching in Ephesus at the school of Tyrannus.
- that the name of Jesus was glorified when the sons of Sceva attempted to use His name as an incantation to ill effect.
- that Christianity caused a riot in Ephesus because worshiping Jesus was likely to damage the idol-making business.
- that perhaps the most important thing Paul did was train disciples who would make disciples.
- that in heading toward Jerusalem, Paul was like Jesus.

Apply this understanding by...

- seeking ways to be discipled and to disciple others as Paul did.

---

mine their whole trade and lead to the great goddess Diana being despised (Acts 19:24-27). As a result, the whole city, riotous and confused, rushed into the theater in anger about the offense against Diana. Of course, Paul and his companions had done nothing wrong, so when the magistrate calmed the crowd down, he told them that if Demetrius and his fellow craftsmen had charges to bring against them, they should do it in a lawful court (Acts 19:35-41). Here is another example of how the preaching of the gospel so fundamentally undermined the pantheistic society and caused chaos, confusion and rioting.

Paul then left Ephesus and went to Macedonia, encouraging the believers along the way (Acts 20:1). He returned through Macedonia and sailed to Troas. While he was teaching in Troas, a young man fell asleep and fell out of a window to his death. Paul rushed to his side and raised him from the dead (Acts 20:10). He then traveled on to Miletus; he didn't want to go back through Ephesus because he was afraid he would be there too long and not make it back to Jerusalem in time for the feast of Pentecost. So he invited the elders from Ephesus to come to visit him in Miletus so that he could bless and encourage them (Acts 20:17). He then departed from Miletus to make his way toward Jerusalem.

totalling in value of up to 50,000 pieces of silver (Acts 19:19).

Following his time in Ephesus, Paul intended to go to Jerusalem and then on to Rome (Acts 19:21). He did eventually go to these places, but not before a great riot in Ephesus.

A silversmith named Demetrius, who made idols for the temple of Diana, called together all the craftsmen of Ephesus and pointed out that the things Paul was teaching were going to under-

On their way toward Jerusalem, Paul and his companions traveled to Cos, then on to Rhodes, then Parara and finally on to Tyre (Acts 21:1). In Tyre, some disciples told Paul through the Holy Spirit not to go to Jerusalem. They traveled next to Ptolemais. Here, a Christian prophet told Paul that if he went to Jerusalem, he would be bound and handed over to the Gentiles. This would make a normal man hesitant to go to Jerusalem, but Paul said, "For I am ready not only to be

bound, but also to die at Jerusalem for the name of the Lord Jesus" (Acts 21:13).

When Paul arrived in Jerusalem, he made peace with the disciples there and was arrested in the temple (Acts 21:33).

Paul—the disciple-maker
Paul is known as an evangelist—bringing the gospel to places it had never gone. And he did a lot of that. We have story after story of him sharing the gospel for the first time ever in synagogues and public places. But if you add up the hours, much more of his time was spent discipling believers and church leaders.

Timothy, Silas, Luke and others all traveled with Paul, both to help him in his ministry and to learn from him. He spent much time in Ephesus training the elders—including a year and a half teaching in the school of Tyrannus. Teaching and training leaders was truly Paul's bread and butter. The gospel doesn't transform society by high-powered evangelists and pastors spreading the gospel in large venues. The gospel transforms the world when disciples make disciples in order to disciple others.

Paul is the new Jesus
Luke 9:51 says that Jesus "steadfastly set His face to go to Jerusalem," knowing that His time to die had come. As He went, He sent out 70 disciples through all the cities to cast out demons and share the gospel.

In Acts 18-21, Paul is like one of the 70 in Luke 10. He went from city to city, casting out demons and sharing the gospel. If he was welcomed in a city, he let his peace rest upon it; if he was rejected, he shook the dust off his feet. And like the 70, he saw the Lord do marvelous things through him.

In another way, Paul was like Jesus. He resolutely set his face toward Jerusalem, even when he knew it could cost him his life; he was ready to die. Furthermore, he was like Jesus, training disciples who would take his place when he went on.

We'll see more about the parallels between Paul and Jesus in the next lesson, but for now, understand the implication here. Paul was a giant of the faith, but he was also just another disciple. We are to follow in the footsteps of Paul as he followed in Jesus' footsteps. This means making disciples who make disciples and being prepared to sacrifice for the greater good of the kingdom. You may not be called to the notoriety that Paul was called to, but exercising your gifts in relationship to the Lord will lead to a life like Jesus'.

ACTIVITIES

1. Journal Time: Discipleship. As evidenced by Paul's and Jesus' lives, discipleship is central to the Christian faith. It is not only an excellent means of spreading the good news, it also helps Christians grow in their faith and learn from one another. Take some time to reflect on your experience with discipleship and how you can more effectively be discipled and disciple others; then answer the questions below.

What is your experience with being discipled? _____

_____

_____

_____

_____

_____

_____

_____

_____

Are you currently being discipled? _____

If not, how can you put yourself in a position to be discipled? _____

_____

_____

_____

_____

_____

_____

_____

_____

Unit 7: The Church Expands

Who are some people you could ask to disciple you? _____
_____
_____
_____
_____

What is your experience with discipling others? _____
_____
_____
_____
_____
_____

Are you currently discipling anyone? _____

If not, is there anyone in your life right now that God may be leading you to disciple? _____
_____
_____
_____

What are some concrete steps you can take to disciple that person? _____
_____
_____
_____

2. Map It. Mark and label Paul's second missionary journey on the blank map on page 87. Use the information in Acts 18:23-21:16 to construct your map.

Lesson 7.4

EVALUATION

1. What did Paul do for two years while in Ephesus on his third missionary journey? _____
_____
_____

2. What happened when the sons of Sceva attempted to use Jesus' name as an incantation to cast out demons? _____
_____
_____
_____
_____

3. What caused the riot in Ephesus during Paul's third missionary journey? _____
_____
_____

4. What is one way Paul was like Jesus? _____
_____
_____
_____
_____

5. What was the most significant thing Paul did on these missionary journeys? _____
_____

LESSON 7.5

Paul's Arrest and Journey to Rome

UNIT 7

NOTES TO THE TEACHER

Lesson Theme - Death, resurrection and the conversion of the Roman Empire

Acts is an unfinished story. At the end of the book, Paul was preaching in Rome. The Roman Empire was in rebellion against God and unbelieving... but we know what happens next. Jesus was arrested and tried in three courts: the Sanhedrin, the Herodian, and the Roman. And as a result, the gospel went out to Jerusalem, Judea and Samaria through His apostles. Likewise, Paul was tried in the same courts: the Sanhedrin and the Herodian, and now he was awaiting his Roman trial. Rome is the new Jerusalem, and Paul was ready to die for the city of man in order to bring the Roman Empire into an encounter with the gospel of our Lord.

In the last lesson, Paul was set on making it to Jerusalem, just like Jesus was when He knew the time of His death had come. Also, like Jesus, Paul knew what was coming. On at least two occasions, disciples in the cities he visited warned him *in the Holy Spirit* that bad things would happen to him in Jerusalem. They were appealing to his sensibilities to not go so that he would be safe; but God wanted him to go, and Paul knew it. He was prepared to be arrested, bound and killed for his faith in Jesus.

Paul arrested in the temple

When Paul arrived in Jerusalem, he was encouraged by the elders to very carefully carry out the purification rite associated with the (presumably) Nazarite vow along with several men who had taken the same vow. Taking part in these purity

OVERVIEW

Paul was the new Jesus. He was arrested in Jerusalem and tried before the Sanhedrin, the local Roman authorities and Herod. But he didn't die in Jerusalem. He was taken to Rome where he was put under house arrest. The book of Acts never tells us the end of Paul's story—to this day, the Church continues the story from where he left off.

SOURCE MATERIAL

- Acts 21:17-28:30

rites would galvanize Paul's reputation among Jews who believed he had simply discarded the Law (Acts 21:20-26). While Paul was in the temple, some Jews cried out to have him seized under the false accusation that he had defiled the temple by bringing Gentiles into it. Pretty soon, the whole town was in a frenzy (Acts 21:30). They dragged Paul out of the temple and were about to kill him when a local Roman military commander stopped them. He had Paul bound and ordered that he be sent to the barracks.

But before being taken to the barracks, Paul asked the commander if he could speak to the people (Acts 21:37). When the commander realized that Paul was a Roman, he let him speak. So Paul got up and told them how the Lord Jesus Christ had saved him on the road to Damascus and called him to bring the gospel to the Gentiles (Acts 22:1-21). Paul built a rebuke into his story, telling of when he had come to Jerusalem after

Unit 7: The Church Expands

OBJECTIVES

Feel...

- impressed with Paul's boldness before crowds that hated him.
- pleased with Paul's shrewdness in turning the Pharisees and Sadducees against each other.
- thankful that God had a plan to reach the Gentiles with the gospel.

Understand...

- the sequence of events from Paul's arrest to his trial before the Sanhedrin and how he used the situation to his advantage.
- that Paul turned the Pharisees and Sadducees against each other.
- that Jesus appeared to Paul, encouraging him to be a witness before Him in Rome.
- that Felix held Paul for two years, trying to figure out what to do with him, and that he often met with Paul to hear about Christianity.
- that since Paul had appealed to Caesar, Festus had to send him on to Rome.
- that like Jesus, Paul had appeared before the Sanhedrin, the local Roman authorities and Herod; but unlike Jesus, Paul was taken to Rome to reach the Gentiles.
- that Acts is an unfinished story because we are still fulfilling Paul's mission.

Apply this understanding by...

- seeking ways to continue the unfinished story of Acts.
- reflecting on how to tell your own story of meeting Jesus.

becoming a Christian and Jesus had appeared to him and told him to leave because he would not be received by those in Jerusalem; instead, Paul's call was far away among the Gentiles.

Paul's words were prophetic on multiple levels. He always had difficulty in Jerusalem. The apostles and elders got along with him well enough, but neither the Jewish Christians nor the Jewish unbelievers in Jerusalem would receive him. Antioch became his home base because he was so well-received there. But that's not all; right after Paul gave his testimony, the crowds rose up in anger, again rejecting his witness (Acts 22:22). And finally, even in bondage, Paul would not be received in Jerusalem, but was taken to Rome where although he would be imprisoned, he would have the freedom to minister the gospel.

The next day, the commander released Paul and had him stand before the Sanhedrin (Acts 22:30), just like Jesus had years before. The Sanhedrin was made up of both Sadducees and Pharisees. When Paul realized that there were both Pharisees and Sadducees there, he decided to turn them against each other so that they would be distracted from him (Acts 23:6). While the Pharisees believed in the resurrection and the existence of spirits and angels, the Sadducees rejected these things. So Paul told the Sanhedrin that he was simply a Pharisee in trouble for believing in the resurrection and spirits (in his testimony, the resurrected Jesus had appeared to him). This turned the Pharisees and Sadducees against each other, and the Pharisees began defending Paul!

The dissension was so great that the commander was afraid Paul (a Roman citizen) would be injured, so he put him in the barracks. Jesus appeared to him that night and said, "Be of good cheer, Paul; for as you have testified for Me in

Jerusalem, so you must also bear witness in Rome" (Acts 23:11). Jesus' words validated both that Paul was in God's will by being arrested in Jerusalem and also that the following events were a part of God's plan.

The plot to murder Paul
Something interesting happened next. The Jews were the ones bringing charges against Paul, and the Romans would often defer to the religious authorities when it came to a matter of Jewish law. But when the Romans found out that Paul was a Roman citizen, they began to *protect* him. While he was in the barracks, a conspiracy formed against him. More than forty Jews took an oath, saying that they wouldn't eat or drink until they had killed Paul (Acts 23:12-13). When Paul heard about the plot, he brought it to the attention of the commander who arranged for Paul to transfer to Caesarea (where he would be tried by Felix) under guard of 200 horsemen (Acts 23:23).

Felix refused to hear Paul's case until his accusers brought charges against him to Caesarea (Acts 23:35). Several days later, Ananias, the high priest, brought charges of sedition against Paul, claiming that he was a creator of dissension among the Jews. Paul responded to these accusations by informing Felix that he believed in the Law, the Prophets and the resurrection of the dead and made the case that he had done nothing to cause offense in the eyes of God and man (Acts 24:16).

Felix gave Paul a lot of freedom, but did not release him. In fact, he held him for two years and regularly had him come into his presence to explain more about Christianity (Acts 24:24-27).

When Felix was succeeded by Festus, the interest in Paul was renewed (Acts 25:2). The Jews tried to petition Festus to send Paul to Jerusalem so they could lie in wait to ambush him; but instead, Festus let some time pass and then called Paul to appear before him. He wanted to do the Jews a favor and send Paul to Jerusalem, but Paul refused and appealed to Caesar (Acts 25:11).

Paul's trial before Herod Agrippa
Jesus had been tried before the Sanhedrin, then before the Roman authorities and finally, before Herod. The same thing was now happening to Paul. After Paul appealed to Caesar, Festus met with Herod Agrippa to try to figure out how to deal with the situation (Acts 25:14). The problem was that no real charges had been presented before Festus; from his perspective, it was just a disagreement between Jewish sects. Paul had appealed to Caesar, which meant that they needed to figure out what the charges against Paul were so they could send Caesar a letter explaining these charges.

So Paul appeared before Herod to explain the charges that the Jews wanted to bring against him and defend himself from them (Acts 25:23). Paul's defense, recorded in Acts 26, is perhaps the most thrilling recounting of the story of Paul's conversion and ministry. The basic outline is as follows: the charge the Jews wished to bring against him was that he was firmly convinced that the hope of the Jews had come to pass. The resurrection had begun in Jesus Christ. Paul had been convinced because Jesus Himself had appeared to him which meant He was alive, and Jesus called Paul to serve Him as Lord, as His resurrection proved that He was. So Paul turned from killing the Christians to discipling the nations for Christ—because the hope of the resurrection was true!

Agrippa found Paul's story compelling and said that he was almost ready to convert to Christianity (Acts 26:28)! He concluded, like Festus had, that Paul had done nothing worthy of death and that if he hadn't appealed to Caesar, he might be set free (Acts 26:32).

Paul's journey to Rome
Despite lacking a good charge against him, Festus and Agrippa sent Paul to Rome to appear before Caesar. They set sail for Rome and came up against a great storm. Paul had warned the sailors that the ship was going to face a disaster if they sailed on, but they continued anyway (Acts 27:10). The storm grew very intense, and they were stranded at sea for nearly two weeks trying to make it to safety. Many hadn't eaten, fearing that they were going to die. But Paul had heard from the Lord that they were going to survive. He encouraged those on the ship and broke bread with thankfulness to God for giving them food to eat (Acts 27:21-26, 33-36).

They finally landed, shipwrecked on the Island of Malta, with the ship greatly damaged. They spent some time on the island, where Paul was able to share the gospel and heal the sick (Acts 28:8-9). After three months, they sailed on in another ship and arrived in Rome, undoubtedly behind schedule, but safe. Paul was permitted to live by himself with a soldier to keep him under guard (Acts 28:16).

He was able to meet with the local Jewish leaders to share the gospel. As was usually the case, a number of them believed, but many did not, and they departed his house in dispute. He remained there for two years under guard, awaiting trial, but freely ministered to all who would come to him.

Epilogue
Acts ends somewhat abruptly, probably because the book was sent out before Paul's trial. What happened at his trial and after isn't exactly clear, but Christian tradition records that he was eventually beheaded by Nero. But Paul did not die before bringing encouragement and strengthening to the Roman church. It would be several hundred years before the seeds he planted throughout the Roman Empire would bear this fruit; but ultimately, Rome would become Christian and form the foundation for a Christianized western civilization.

Another lesson that we can take away from Acts ending so abruptly is that *the job isn't done yet*. Paul carried out Jesus' mission, and we continue in the same trajectory, making disciples of the nations.

APPLICATION

We can learn many things from the life of Paul, but one of the most important lessons is how to live in affliction. Psalm 34:19 says, "Many are the afflictions of the righteous, but the LORD delivers him out of them all." The story of Acts is a story of Paul being delivered out of afflictions, so many times beaten, stoned, and bound... and so many times freed.

There are two important things you'll want to take away from this. First of all, God is good even in our afflictions, and in many ways afflictions are a part of everyone's life. Paul was able to live with gratitude in much and in little, and we should too.

Unit 7: The Church Expands

However, and this is the second thing you'll want to understand, God doesn't visit the same level of suffering on everyone. Paul had a special calling to the Gentiles and a special calling to a life of suffering (Acts 9:15-16). His was a life of really high highs and really low lows. But God has not called us all to the same level of suffering. In other words, don't walk away from the story of Paul believing that the worst thing that can happen will happen because God just loves to bring suffering to Christians. First of all, that's not even true for Paul; he suffered a lot, but so often, he was delivered before the worst part happened. Secondly, we are not Paul and everyone's calling is different. We are to fear God, but not to be afraid of Him as though He is a tyrant out to hurt us... even if it is for our good. God is good! He loves His people, and He loves to bless with good and perfect gifts; He is good even when life gets hard, which it inevitably will.

Paul's witness before Agrippa is a powerful example of how Christian witness should work. Paul simply told the story of how he met and got to know Jesus. Paul's story was particularly compelling because it was so miraculous, but it was also compelling because Paul really believed that he *knew* Jesus Christ.

Our ability to witness effectively is aided greatly by actually knowing and walking with Jesus and telling the story of our relationship with Him so that it comes across that we really do *know* Him. If we know Jesus, that means that Jesus has risen from the dead, which means that there is hope for the resurrection of the world. This is good news to anyone who will believe.

ACTIVITIES

1. Finish the Story. Acts is an unfinished story. Paul went to Rome and was under house arrest, but ministered the gospel to many visitors. We never hear about what happened to Paul in Rome. Of course, from Church history we know he was martyred, but Acts ends mid-story for a purpose. It is our story, and it's not finished yet. Read through Matthew 28:18-20 and Acts 1:8 and answer the questions below.

Name five things that Paul did throughout his ministry to fulfill Jesus' commissions from Matthew 28:18-20 and Acts 1:8. _____

_____
_____
_____
_____
_____
_____

Lesson 7.5

How many of those things are you presently doing? _____
_____
_____
_____

How many are you not presently doing that you are capable of doing? _____
_____
_____
_____
_____
_____

What would it take to start doing them? _____
_____
_____
_____

Which things are you not presently able to do? Why not? _____
_____
_____
_____
_____

Write a prayer asking God to guide you in your efforts to reach your neighbors. _____
_____
_____
_____
_____
_____
_____

Unit 7: The Church Expands

2. Journal Time: Your Story. Paul used the story of his conversion over and over again when he had the chance to speak to unbelievers in a public forum. He did this because it demonstrated that Jesus was alive—Paul had actually met Jesus and been set free.

Do you have a story of meeting Jesus? We are not simply asking about when you got saved. Maybe that's your story of meeting Jesus, but many people don't really meet Him in a deep and personal way until they are going through a hard time and He steps in to speak to them. If you do have a story, write the short version of it below as though you are telling it to an unbeliever._____

_____
_____
_____
_____
_____
_____
_____
_____
_____
_____
_____
_____
_____

If you haven't met Jesus, write a short prayer asking Him to show Himself to you in an unmistakable and deeply personal way._____

_____
_____
_____

3. Map It. Mark and label Paul's arrest and journey to Rome on the blank map on page 98. Use the information in Acts 18:23-21:16 to construct your map.

Lesson 7.5

EVALUATION

1. What was the "official" reason that Paul was arrested in Jerusalem? _____
_____
_____

2. What did Paul seek to do as soon as he was arrested? _____
_____
_____

3. How did Paul go about preaching the gospel? _____
_____

4. Why do you think Paul used his own story to share the gospel?_____
_____
_____
_____

5. Jesus was tried before three different authorities: the Sanhedrin, the Roman authorities and Herod. How many of these same authorities was Paul tried before? _____

6. In what way did Paul's story differ from Jesus'? _____
_____
_____

7. What compelled the Roman military to take Paul to Caesarea?_____
_____

9. What did Paul do to get himself transferred to Rome?_____
_____

  How does Acts end? _____
_____

10. Why do you think Acts ends this way?_____
_____

END OF YEAR ACTIVITIES

1. **Highs and Lows.** The Story of God's people is filled with highs and lows. Draw a graph of the New Testament Story. Begin with a horizontal timeline of the Story from Jesus' birth to Paul's house arrest in Rome. Then add a vertical axis, charting the lowest, most discouraging points in the Story at the bottom and the most blessed high points at the very top. If it helps, you can subdivide this activity into two sections (the life of Jesus and the early Church).

2. **The Spread of the Gospel.** Get a large world map that you can write on. Chart the geographical spread of the gospel, starting with Pentecost and working through the dispersions and missionary journeys of the New Testament. When you get done with the New Testament, point out where you are on the map. How'd that happen? Think through how the gospel came to be everywhere it is today.

3. **Your Gospel Genealogy.** Map your own gospel genealogy back as far as you can. Who is primarily responsible for telling you about Jesus? Of course, we don't know the names, but our genealogies all go back to someone who was there at Pentecost, and from there to Jesus. Jesus told someone about Himself, and that person told someone else, and so on for 2,000 years, down to the names we still remember. Join the story and become part of someone else's gospel genealogy

www.ingramcontent.com/pod-product-compliance
Lightning Source LLC
Chambersburg PA
CBHW081337080526
44588CB00017B/2656